BOLD AS LOVE
The Jimi Hendrix Experience

Frank Moriarty

MetroBooks

MetroBooks

An Imprint of Friedman/Fairfax Publishers

© 1996 by Michael Friedman Publishing Group, Inc.

Library of Congress Cataloging-in-Pubication data
available upon request.

ISBN 1-56799-385-0

Editor: Stephen Slaybaugh
Art Director: Lynne Yeamans
Design: Elan Studio
Photography Editor: Dorian Romer
Production Director: Karen Matsu Greenberg

Color separations by Bright Arts Graphics (S) Pte Ltd
Printed in China by Leefung-Asco Printers Ltd

For bulk purchases and special sales, please contact:
Friedman/Fairfax Publishers
Attention: Sales Department
15 West 26th Street
New York, NY 10010
(212) 685-6610 • FAX (212) 685-1307

Visit the Friedman/Fairfax Website:
http://www.webcom.com/friedman

CONTENTS

acknowledgments

Thanks to Noel Redding, for reading the text carefully and offering his corrections, recollections, and insight into his days with The Jimi Hendrix Experience. To have had one of the musicians I saw perform with Jimi read through my work twenty-five years later was a unique thrill.

At the Michael Friedman Publishing Group, thanks to Sharyn Rosart and Michael Friedman for giving me the opportunity to participate in this project. Stephen Slaybaugh was a pleasure to work with as this book's editor, and his suggestions and willingness to listen to my ideas are appreciated. Dorian Romer did a great job as photo editor in tracking down seldom-seen imagery of Jimi Hendrix, and Lori Thorn's design has provided a perfect setting for the story of Jimi and his music.

Mitchell Mercurio has proofread much of my work over the years, and his sharp eyes and suggestions are always welcome. This book has benefited from his efforts.

Thanks to David Goerk, Michael McGeffigan, and Tom Sheehy for the use of their Hendrix-related materials and for their interest and support.

The Jimi Hendrix mailing list on the Internet keeps the memory of Jimi alive and revels in the excitement of his music every day with interesting comments and exchanges of opinions about rock's greatest guitarist. (For more information, e-mail hey-joe-request@inslab.uky.edu with "subscribe" as subject.)

Finally, thanks to Caesar Glebbeek, scholar of the music of Jimi and publisher of *UniVibes: The International Jimi Hendrix Magazine.* Through Caesar's efforts, documentation of Jimi's life is preserved and updated, providing a valuable service to all lovers of the music of Jimi Hendrix.

Dedication

This book is dedicated with love to my wife, Portia, whose support, advice, and ideas helped make this a better book. Aside from the usual eccentricities encountered when one of my book projects is under way, she has doubtlessly heard more music by Jimi Hendrix than she ever imagined. I'm grateful for her patience and encouragement.

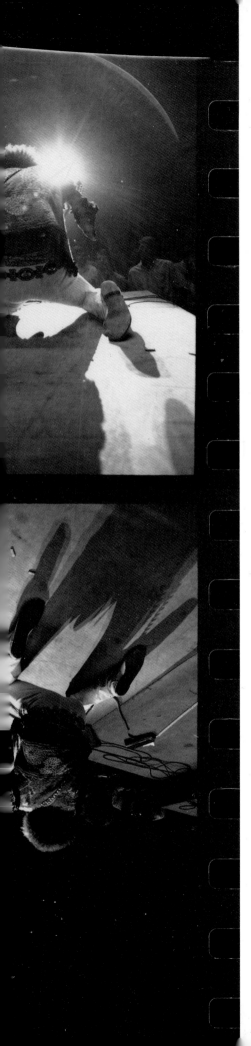

PREFACE

I first met Jimi Hendrix auditioning to be the bass player in his new band, even though I had only played six-string before then. The session consisted of Jimi playing chords—no vocals—while I attempted to learn the bass on the spot. I think even then I somehow felt that the guy had something special. ❧ When we were through, Jimi invited me to the pub up the road. We had a pint of bitter, which Jimi liked. We discussed music. I found Hendrix to be very quiet and polite. He wanted to know more about the English music scene and I wanted to know about the American scene. After we finished our beers, Jimi asked me if I would join his group! ❧ For three long years we toured hard, recorded albums, and did television and radio spots. We were very young and I think it was a real "experience" for all of us. Even though Jimi was the heart of the band, I still like to think that he couldn't have accomplished everything he did without the help of Mitch, Chas, and myself. ❧ Now, twenty-five years later, I'm still amazed and flattered that the music of The Jimi Hendrix Experience is still revered, even though Jimi's no longer with us (God bless him). I feel honored just to have been able to play with him and I hope that wherever he is, he's happy that our music is still alive.

Noel Redding
Prague, November 1995

FOREWORD

I first saw Jimi Hendrix at the Spectrum in Philadelphia in April 1969. The church my parents belonged to, attempting to connect with the younger generation, decided it would be a good idea to take members of the church's youth group to see Jimi Hendrix. Maybe the fact that this tour was christened *Electric Church* helped make up their minds, but all I knew was that this was the only way I'd be able to see the most important musician in my young life. ❧ So I found myself, at the age of thirteen, sitting in the next-to-last row of a twenty-thousand-seat arena waiting to see Jimi Hendrix. ❧ I was in the building, but definitely not close enough. So, after Noel Redding's band, Fat Mattress, had performed their opening set, I took advantage of my "just a kid" status to worm my way deep onto the floor of the Spectrum. Closer and closer I edged toward the stage, wondering when that grown-up hand would grab my shoulder and banish me back to the rafters. That hand never came. ❧ I made it all the way to the sixth row, where a kindly hippie girl let me stand on her chair to witness The Jimi Hendrix Experience. What I saw and heard that night irrevocably changed my life. ❧ Jimi Hendrix is still changing lives decades later, and his status as one of the most important musicians in our culture's history becomes more secure with each passing year. I never had the opportunity to express my gratitude to Jimi for his music, but if this book helps expose new listeners to the work of Jimi Hendrix, then writing it is my chance to say, "Thank you."

CHAPTER ONE

BEGINNINGS

Jimi Hendrix was a human being.

A simple fact, but one that seems to have been forgotten in the years since rock and roll's most influential guitarist died in 1970. Like Elvis Presley or Marilyn Monroe, Jimi Hendrix has risen to that strange plane of cultural existence where he is seen more as a collection of images and sound bites than as a living, breathing person.

But to perceive Jimi as nothing more than an icon or a symbol of a period of time is to forget that Jimi was funny, and sometimes shy. He could get exasperated, or become frustrated with his work. An avid reader of science fiction, he kept a diary of his adventures as well. Jimi wrote letters to his family. He enjoyed eating soup. He was loyal to his friends, and curious and open to new ideas. In those aspects, he was like many other people. But, of course, there was one big difference: Jimi Hendrix played guitar like no other human being before or since.

It's that last fact that is responsible for the rarified atmosphere his legend continues to live in. With each passing year the memory of Jimi Hendrix the person yields to Jimi Hendrix the legend.

The story of the man named Jimi Hendrix begins with the birth of a child to Al and Lucille Jeter Hendrix. The marriage of Lucille and Al was far from stable, and Al—who had been drafted into the army—was stationed in Alabama when Lucille gave birth to Johnny Allen Hendrix at King County Hospital in Seattle, Washington.

November 27, 1942, was the day the future of the electric guitar and rock and roll were irrevocably altered. A child primarily of African-American descent, Johnny also inherited Cherokee Indian bloodlines from Al's mother, Nora.

During his early years, Johnny lived in an atmosphere of near-constant family turmoil. Al tried to file for divorce from Lucille just after Johnny's birth, and Lucille made it clear that caring for a baby was not a top priority for her. In fact, the infant's name, Johnny Allen, was chosen by Lucille as a representation of the two men in her life: her husband, James Allen Hendrix, and her boyfriend, John Williams. Lucille was known to drink too much and disappear for days at a time.

Johnny was shuttled about between members of Lucille's family, Al's family, and various friends. He suffered through a bout of pneumonia at the age of six months, but was fairly healthy despite living a rootless existence with a revolving cast of caretakers. Finally, just after Johnny turned three years old, Al Hendrix returned to Seattle from his obligations with the armed forces, which had entailed a lengthy stint in the Fiji Islands.

Almost immediately Al traveled to Berkeley, California, to collect his son from a friend of the Jeter family named Mrs. Champ. After returning to Seattle, Al and Johnny stayed with Al's sister-in-law, Dolores Jeter. During this period Al unsuccessfully attempted to discourage his son's natural left-handed tendencies, a common practice at the time. And although he would one day be world-renowned for his abilities on the guitar, Johnny, at the age of four, received his first musical instrument—a harmonica.

On September 11, 1946, Johnny Allen's name was changed to James Marshall Hendrix. Al Hendrix was not pleased with the name Lucille bestowed upon his son, and chose James Marshall in honor of his brother, Leon Marshall, who had died in 1932. From that point on, the child was known as Jimmy.

When she learned that Al had returned from the army, Lucille sought him out and a short-lived reconciliation took place—long enough for Jimmy to gain two younger brothers. Leon was born on January 13, 1948, and Joseph Allen followed a year later. But the relationship between Al and Lucille was tempestuous and off-and-on at best.

In mid-1949, Al—now working as a laborer and gardener—sent Jimmy and Leon to live with his sister Patricia and her husband, Joe Lachley, in Vancouver, Canada. But Joe passed away in early 1950, and Patricia and the two boys soon headed back to Seattle.

Jimmy attended a variety of public schools and already displayed a growing interest in the guitar. He would take a broomstick and imagine it was the real thing, holding it across his body as he manipulated imaginary strings. Jimmy's interest was so great that, when he was eight years old and attending the Horace Mann Elementary School in Seattle, a social worker tried to convince the school to buy Jimmy a real guitar with funds intended for financial hardships. But the request was turned down, and Jimmy had to wait for his first guitar.

Lucille and Al Hendrix had a daughter in September 1950, but Cathy Ira was adopted almost immediately. Soon after, Al and Lucille's troubled marriage ended in divorce. Al was awarded custody of Jimmy, Leon, and Joseph, but Joseph was also

adopted shortly thereafter. Jimmy was ten years old; Leon was five. Al had trouble finding work, and the splintered family lived in difficult circumstances.

Despite living in poverty, many aspects of Jimmy's childhood were like those of most children. At the suggestion of an aunt, Jimmy and his best friend, James Williams, joined the Boy Scouts. And they each had paper routes. Al often took the kids to the movies, where Jimmy became fascinated by the heroics of Flash Gordon. Jimmy also began to play football in a youth league.

But Al's employment and financial troubles were continuing, and Jimmy and Leon were both regularly switching schools and addresses as their father moved throughout the Seattle area. By late 1956, Al was forced to give Leon up to foster care. Jimmy stayed with his father and during this time had two brushes with famous musicians: he saw Elvis Presley perform on September 1, 1957, in Seattle, and he met Little Richard, who would one day hire Jimmy as a guitarist. Little Richard Penniman's mother lived nearby and knew Al and Jimmy, and arranged the meeting when she heard how crazy Jimmy was about music.

Meanwhile, Lucille Jeter Hendrix remarried after the divorce from Al, taking vows with William Mitchell on January 3, 1958. Jimmy had visited his mother during a hospital stay in 1957, but that was the last time he saw her alive. Less than a month after taking her new husband, Lucille died of a ruptured spleen—a complication from years of heavy drinking. Al, Jimmy, and Leon did not attend the funeral.

In the summer of 1958, Jimmy finally got his first guitar, which was bought from a friend of Al's for five dollars. Jimmy soon discovered he had a lot to learn.

"I didn't know that I would have to turn the strings around the other way because I was left-handed," he recalled years later, "but it just didn't feel right. I can remember thinking to myself, 'There's something wrong here....' I changed the strings around but it was way out of tune when I'd finished. I didn't know a thing about tuning so I went down to the store and run my fingers across the strings on a guitar they had there. After that I got tired of the guitar and put it aside."

Fortunately for the world of music, Chuck Berry re-ignited Jimmy's interest in the guitar and Hendrix joined his first band, The Velvetones, in 1958. But Jimmy faced an immediate problem—he was drowned out by the electric guitars of the other musicians. Al bought Jimmy his first electric guitar a year later. Armed with the Supro guitar, Jimmy chose the "Peter Gunn" theme as one of his first musical conquests.

After joining a new band, The Rocking Kings, Jimmy made his first appearance on stage with an electric guitar in 1959. The venue was a National Guard armory near Kent, Washington. But following a Rocking Kings gig in 1960, Jimmy's Supro was stolen. Eventually, Al gave in and bought Jimmy a new electric guitar, this time a Danelectro.

Jimi left high school in the twelfth grade after failing to graduate from Garfield High School. When not consumed with the guitar and his new band, Thomas and the Tomcats, Jimmy helped Al with landscape gardening.

"He had a not-so-good running contracting firm," recalled Hendrix of his father, "and in me he saw a cheap laborer. I didn't see it that way. I had to carry stones and cement all day, and he pocketed the money."

With poor job prospects clouding his future, in April 1961, at the age of eighteen, Jimmy volunteered for the army. A draft notice would surely be headed his way eventually, and by volunteering Jimmy was able to choose his fate. Jimmy Hendrix became a "Screaming Eagle," a paratrooper with the 101st Airborne Division.

Just before his nineteenth birthday, Jimmy arrived in Ford Ord, Kentucky—farther from his home than he had ever travelled. While battling homesickness and enduring jump school, Jimmy turned to his guitar for solace. While playing one night, Jimmy made a new friend—a bass player named Billy Cox. Cox heard Hendrix playing and, intrigued by the sounds, walked up and introduced himself. Soon after, Cox and Hendrix teamed up to play in various service clubs. It was to be the beginning of a lengthy musical partnership.

During his twenty-sixth paratrooper jump in May 1962, Jimmy broke his right ankle. On July 2 at Fort Campbell, Jimmy was discharged from the army for medical reasons. Hendrix and Cox had performed in clubs like the Pink Poodle in nearby Clarkesville, Tennessee, and that was where Jimmy decided to wait out the two months Billy Cox still had to serve in the army.

Cox and Hendrix labored away in small bands for the rest of 1962, eventually migrating to Nashville. After a brief sojourn in Vancouver to visit his grandmother Nora, Jimmy headed south to begin a lengthy period of paying dues. He played with blues musician Slim Harpo in Mississippi in early 1963 before heading back to Tennessee. Once there, Hendrix was reunited in a succession of bands with Billy Cox and guitarist Larry Lee.

"Around this time, people nicknamed Jimmy 'Marbles,' because he walked up the street with an electric guitar, playing it," Cox told Guitar Player's Jas Obrecht in 1989. "He'd play it in the show, he'd play it coming back from the gig. I saw him put 25 years into the guitar in five years, because it was a constant, everyday occurrence with him. People called him Marbles because they thought he was crazy. They couldn't understand why a man would constantly be playing a guitar all the time....

"I remember mornings waking Jimmy up, knocking on his door, and there he was laying on the bed with the same clothes he had on the night before, his guitar laying on his stomach or alongside him," Cox continued. "He was practicing all night long."

"You really had to play, because those people were really hard to please," Hendrix recalled.

Above, left and right: The showmanship that Hendrix displayed with the Experience was developed during years of paying dues with other performers, who often were not pleased about being upstaged by a backing musician. These two 1965 photographs show Jimi with Curtis Knight and the Squires in New York City clubs, dressed in white at the Queen's Inn and in black at the Purple Onion. In each photo Hendrix is on the left with Knight in the center. Knight recognized Jimi's talent and gave him more leeway to step out musically. Opposite: Jimi, now at the command of his own band, displays his musical prowess.

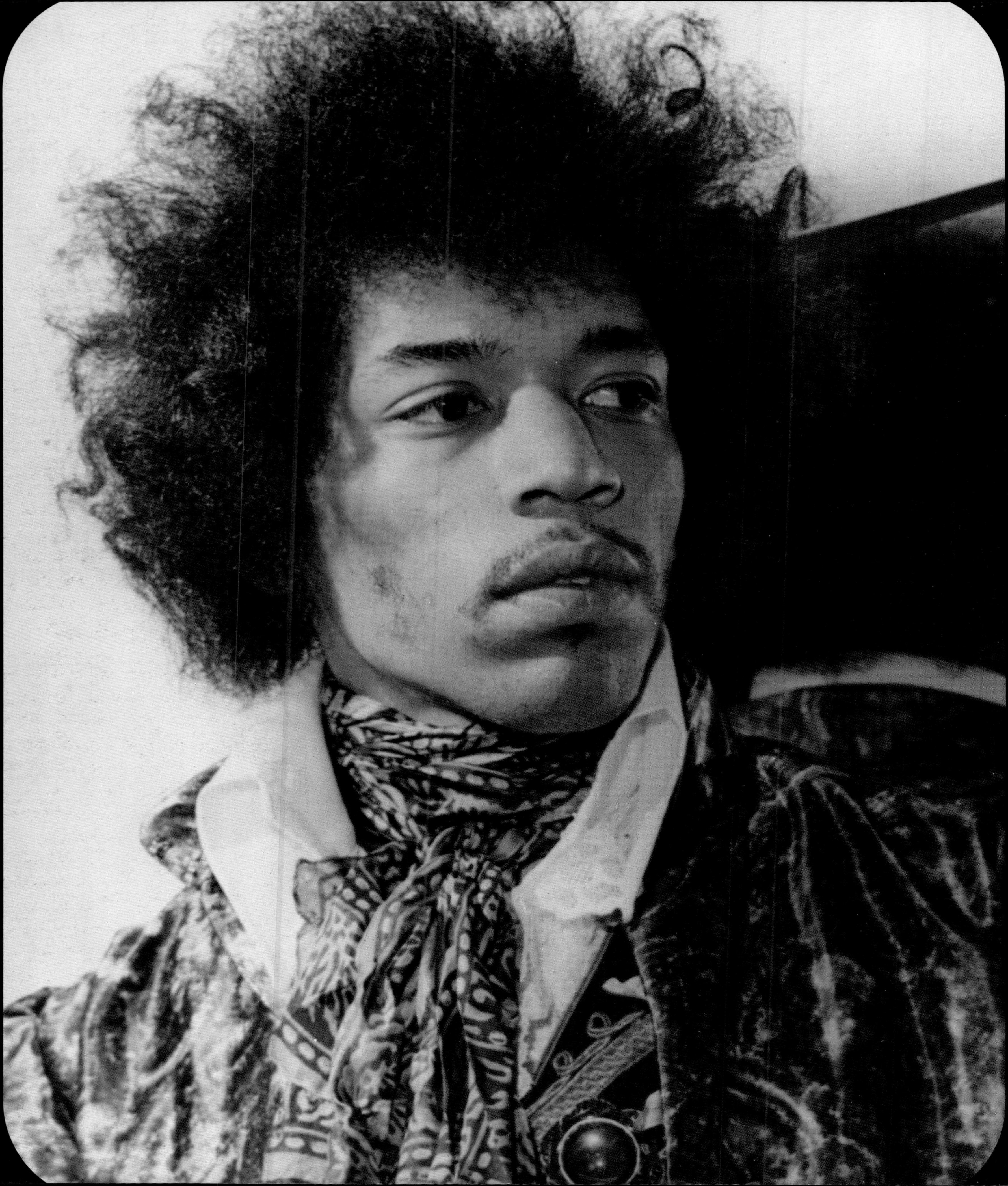

"It was one of the hardest audiences in the South; they hear it all the time. Everybody knows how to play guitar. You walk down the street and people are sitting on their porch playing more guitar. That's where I learned to play, really, in Nashville."

Not content to remain in Tennessee, Hendrix decided to try his luck up north. On his way to New York late in 1963, Jimmy met Lonnie Youngblood in Philadelphia and played his first official studio date. This resulted in the first records bearing the guitar playing of Jimmy Hendrix: "Go Go Shoes" b/w "Go Go Place," a single released on Fairmount Records late in 1963, and a second Fairmount release early in 1964 of "Soul Food" and "Goodbye Bessie Mae." Of course, both records were released under Youngblood's name with no mention of the unknown guitarist.

A brief stint with the Isley Brothers followed before Jimmy wound up as a tour guitarist for "Gorgeous" George Odell on package tours that gathered stars like Sam Cooke and Jackie Wilson for grueling performance itineraries throughout the South. Jimmy acquired his first Fender guitar—a Jazzmaster—late in 1964, and the guitar accompanied him as he toured behind Little Richard, a gig arranged for Hendrix by Odell.

Except for a brief period playing in the Ike and Tina Turner Review, Jimmy stayed with Little Richard until the middle of 1965, playing backing guitar and following the band's strict dress code. Little Richard was a flamboyant performer, and Hendrix was left with little opportunity to display his burgeoning talent. In an interview in 1967, Hendrix recalled his stint with the mercurial rock and roll pioneer.

"I had these dreams that something was going to happen, seeing the number 1966 in my sleep,

so I was just passing time until then," Hendrix stated. "I wanted my own scene, making my music, not playing the same riffs."

"Like once with Little Richard, me and another guy got fancy shirts 'cause we were tired of wearing the uniform. Richard called a meeting. 'I am Little Richard, I am Little Richard,' he said, 'the King, the King of Rock and Rhythm, I am the only one allowed to be pretty. Take off those shirts!' Man, it was all like that. Bad pay, lousy living, and getting burned."

The pay may have been bad, but at least there was pay. When Hendrix quit Richard's band in New York, he found himself with no source of income and was even forced to pawn his guitar. Salvation came in the form of singer Curtis Knight, who hired Hendrix into his band and gave him a Fender Duo-Sonic guitar.

Hendrix picked up session work with Knight as part of Knight's band The Squires, and even recorded a song called "Suey" with Jayne Mansfield. But road work provided the best opportunity to make money, and Hendrix spent November 1965 touring with Joey Dee and The Starlighters.

Jimmy Hendrix finished the year 1965 as a member of Curtis Knight and The Squires, performing in Hackensack, New Jersey. Hendrix claimed that he had dreams that 1966 would be his year, but as he stood on the stage of St. George's Club 20, it's doubtful that Hendrix could have ever imagined just how much was in store for him in the year to come. The years of paying dues while backing jealous employers threatened by Hendrix's immense musical talent were about to come to an end.

Opposite: The well-dressed rock star in an outfit that might not have gone over well with Jimi's commanders in the 101st Airborne. Above: Once stardom arrived, visits home to Seattle were infrequent. Jimi and Al are pictured on September 6, 1968, when the Experience were in town for a performance at the Center Coliseum during the band's second major U.S. tour of 1968.

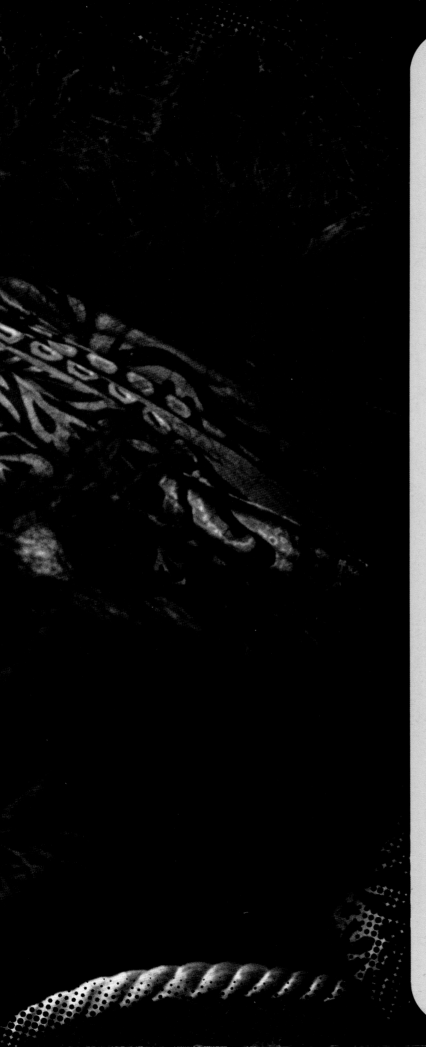

CHAPTER TWO

ASSEMBLING AN EXPERIENCE

The year 1966 began much as 1965 had ended, with Jimmy Hendrix gaining short-term employment as a backing musician. This time sax legend King Curtis benefited from Jimmy's talents, and the union lasted for five months. Jimmy played with Curtis' other guitarist, Cornell Dupree, behind both Curtis and in one-off performances with other acts like Chuck Berry and Wilson Pickett. By May, though, Jimmy was back with Curtis Knight and The Squires.

Soon rock and roll music would undergo a tremendous upheaval, but in 1966 the groundwork for these dramatic changes was being laid. Ken Weaver, a member of the experimental band The Fuggs, liked to toy with electronics. One of Weaver's contraptions was an early fuzz box, designed to distort an electric guitar signal while providing more note sustain. Jimmy was acquainted with Weaver and began to use one of Weaver's fuzz boxes as early as May 1966.

Jimmy's growing talents and creativity, sparked in part by the new sounds he was able to craft with guitar effects, found Hendrix frustrated with the role of sideman. He quit Curtis Knight's band after

a show on May 20 at the Club Cheetah on Broadway in New York, and found another position with Carl Holmes and The Commanders, which proved to be equally stifling to his vision. Hendrix began to toy with the idea of forming his own band.

"I just got tired where I just couldn't stand any more," Hendrix said in 1967. "So I just went down to the Village and got my own little group together named The Rainflowers, you know. We had two names, The Rainflowers and The Blue Flames, you know, any one of those names was all right."

Heavily influenced by Bob Dylan, and soaking up as many opportunities to jam in the clubs of Greenwich Village as possible, Hendrix's musical mind was wide open to new possibilities. He began to explore those options when he landed a regular gig at Cafe Wha? on MacDougal Street. Hendrix finally settled on the name Jimmy James and The Blue Flames, and—armed with a new white Fender Stratocaster—Hendrix and his mates played songs like "Wild Thing," "Like a Rolling Stone," "Killing Floor," "Shotgun," and "Hey Joe" six nights a week. Hendrix had become especially enamored of the last song when he heard Tim Rose's version of it playing on a jukebox in the Village.

The lineup of The Blue Flames was anything but stable, but it was centered around two musicians named Randy, one of whom was from California and the other from Texas. Jimmy promptly dubbed them Randy Texas and Randy California. Randy California later went on to form the well-known band Spirit. An occasional Blue Flame member who also went on to greater things was Jeff Baxter, who would contribute guitar to both Steely Dan and The Doobie Brothers later in his career.

Jimmy was leading The Blue Flames through a set at the Club Cheetah when he was spotted by an observer who would change his life.

On June 23, The Rolling Stones arrived in New York to begin a tour. Traveling with them was Linda Keith, who was Keith

Richards' girlfriend. Linda happened to see Hendrix and The Blue Flames, and was enthralled by the guitarist. She decided to do whatever she could to spread the word about "Jimmy James."

While the Stones toured, Linda Keith stayed behind in New York. She persuaded one record producer to go see Hendrix, but he was less than thrilled with what he heard. Then The Animals came to town.

After several hit records, tensions within The Animals were leading to the breakup of the band. A final tour of the United States was planned, and The Animals hit New York on July 4, 1966. Playing bass with the band was Chas Chandler. Linda Keith not only knew Chandler, she also knew that Chandler was interested in managing and producing acts rather than performing. Chandler was planning on starting a business relationship with The Animals' manager, Mike Jeffery, once the breakup of The Animals was complete at the end of the tour. Keith thought she had a perfect first client for Chandler—Jimmy Hendrix.

Opposite: By the end of 1966, Jimi was armed with the Experience and ready to bring his artistic visions to reality. Above, right: Once he made the journey to England, Jimi could look back and laugh at the days of keeping his hair neat and wearing suits, as in this publicity photo (above, left) of Curtis Knight and The Squires that was distributed by Ed Chalpin's PPX Enterprises in 1966.

Following The Animals' Central Park show, Chas Chandler remained in New York and spent four days just trying to track Jimmy down. Hendrix was surprised that Chandler had actually returned, but Chandler began to put the wheels in motion to get Hendrix over to England. One thing Chandler had already decided was the name of his new client's band: The Jimmy Hendrix Experience.

Chas Chandler spent days trying to buy out all the contracts Jimmy had signed during his stay in New York. Unfortunately, Hendrix forgot to mention one contract signed with Ed Chalpin and his recording company, PPX Enterprises, during his days with Curtis Knight. This oversight would rear its ugly head in the months to come.

Keith took Chandler to Cafe Wha? on July 5 to meet Jimmy and see the band. Chandler was impressed, but the next day he had to leave New York to begin The Animals' tour. Chandler would not return until The Animals' final show of the tour in Central Park on September 5. Before leaving, Chas asked Jimmy if he'd be interested in coming to England and setting up a new base of operations, with his own band and a recording contract. The promise of an introduction to Eric Clapton was what captured Hendrix's attention the most.

Chandler asked Hendrix if he had signed any recording or management contracts, and Jimmy admitted that he had. In truth, Jimmy had signed anything put in front of him if it allowed him to record or get paid. Chandler needed to know who he would have to buy out to avoid future complications. Chandler promised to return at the conclusion of The Animals' tour, but Hendrix was skeptical.

Jimmy wasn't idle in the intervening weeks, forming a band with noted blues musician John Hammond, Jr., and impressing the likes of Al Kooper and Michael Bloomfield. Hendrix was slowly building a reputation.

Meanwhile, Jimmy applied for a passport, which was issued on September 23, 1966. That night Chandler and Hendrix departed for London on a Pan Am flight from New York's JFK International Airport. One final bit of image tuning took place shortly thereafter—Jimmy became known as Jimi.

Upon arrival at London's Heathrow Airport on September 24, Hendrix was issued a nonwork permit after Chandler concocted a story that Jimi was a noted songwriter coming to England to collect royalties.

From the airport, Chandler immediately indoctrinated Hendrix into the London music scene by driving straight to the home of Zoot Money. Money was a noted keyboard player who, much like John Mayall, was known for discovering great musicians. Unfortunately, most of Money's Big Roll Band's equipment was at the site of a gig. So Jimi Hendrix's first British performance was an unplugged one, with the confirmed witnesses being Chandler, Money, Money's wife-to-be, Ronnie, and Money's guitarist, Andy Summers, who would one day found The Police.

Above: Jimi dreamed of being able to play whatever he wanted to, however he wanted to. To develop a following he took his stage stunts to an extreme, incorporating guitar acrobatics to complement his flourishing musical ability. Opposite: Hendrix gets down and dirty at the Blue Moon nite club in

That night Hendrix made his first public appearance on European soil, jamming at the packed Scotch of St. James club in London. Jimi got in a few licks at the popular and influential nightspot before Chas, nervous about Hendrix's nonworking immigration status, discouraged Jimi from further demonstrations of his musical ability. The crowd seemed stunned by what they had seen, but more importantly from Jimi's standpoint, Hendrix met Kathy Etchingham, a friend of Ronnie Money's who would be Jimi's girlfriend in the months to come.

After attending auditions for Eric Burdon's New Animals, which Chas was helping out with, Hendrix and Chandler returned to the Scotch of St. James on September 27, where Jimi jammed with The VIPs. In the crowd were the managers of The Who, Kit Lambert and Chris Stamp. They had plans for starting their own label called Track Records, which would be distributed by Polydor. Lambert and Stamp sought out Chandler and began several weeks of negotiations aimed at bringing The Jimi Hendrix Experience into the Track fold.

No one seemed too alarmed that The Jimi Hendrix Experience, at this point, consisted of just Jimi. After Jimi received the proper certification allowing him stay in England until at least the end of the year, Chandler and Hendrix set about the task of assembling the rest of the Experience.

On September 29, guitarist Noel Redding turned up at the Birdland Club, where Burdon and Chandler were holding auditions for the New Animals. Redding was nearly twenty-one, and had played with The Lonely Ones and The Loving Kind on the British equivalent of the "chitlin circuit." Redding hoped a slot in the New Animals might be his big chance.

Told the New Animals position was already filled, Redding was then asked by Chandler if he might be interested in playing bass with a new American guitar player. Noel borrowed a bass from Chandler and sat in with Jimi, pianist Mike O'Neill, and drummer

Opposite: Jimi was fully at ease with a guitar in his hands, but vocals were another matter. Despite possessing an expressive voice, Jimi doubted his singing abilities and would often chase onlookers away when he recorded vocal tracks in the studio. Above, left and right: A contrast between Jimi's early days of flamboyance and his appearance at later concerts. Although Jimi eventually became loath to perform guitar stunts on demand, flashes of showmanship still characterized his performances.

Aynsley Dunbar. After running through songs including "Hey Joe" and "Have Mercy on Me Baby," Jimi and Noel talked at a nearby pub. Noel was asked to return to the Birdland Club the next day.

But when he turned up the next day, Noel found the Birdland Club deserted. Redding headed over to see Michael Jeffery, Chandler's business partner, at their office. Jeffery offered Redding the job as bassist for the Experience, and days later Chandler confirmed for Noel that the gig was indeed his. The Jimi Hendrix Experience was two-thirds complete.

Meanwhile, Jimi had realized his goal of meeting Eric Clapton. Indeed, Hendrix took up an invitation to show his stuff and made a high-profile splash by performing "Killing Floor" during a prominent London show by Clapton's band Cream on October 1. Clapton was one of the first of Britain's star guitarists to get a close-up look at the bold new talent who would re-invent the use of the electric guitar.

Although Hendrix and Redding had rehearsed with Aynsley Dunbar, nothing was finalized and a full-time drummer was needed. As fate would have it, Georgie Fame and The Blue Flames, possessors of two number one hits, broke up on October 3. The next day The Blue Flames' drummer, Mitch Mitchell, and Chandler discussed the opening with the Hendrix group.

Mitchell, who had abandoned a promising acting career in favor of a string of gigs leading up to his stint with The Blue Flames, turned up at the Birdland Club on October 5. After several hours of running through soul and R&B standards, Mitch was thanked for coming. Chandler has stated that the decision to hire either Mitchell or Dunbar was made in the most logical way possible—they flipped a coin. Mitchell's side came up. The Jimi Hendrix Experience was complete.

The first order of business was to prepare for four concert dates in France, which Chandler had arranged for the coming week. The Jimi Hendrix Experience would be one of several acts supporting French pop star Johnny Hallyday, and their sets would only be about fifteen minutes in length. The day before leaving for Paris, Hendrix, Redding, and Mitchell signed publishing and management contracts with Chas Chandler and Mike Jeffery.

On October 12, The Jimi Hendrix Experience arrived in Paris to begin their first-ever tour. The Novelty cinema in Evreux was the site of the first Experience show, and the threesome filled their

Opposite: Jimi ponders the future at an early Experience photo shoot. Top: Jimi with Eric Clapton. The two guitarists became good friends, so much so that when Jimi died Clapton switched from Gibson guitars to Fender Stratocasters like Hendrix's in tribute to his memory. Above: Hendrix and Noel Redding at work in the studio.

fifteen minutes with songs including "Respect," "Everybody Needs Somebody to Love," "Land of a Thousand Dances," "Midnight Hour," and "Have Mercy on Me Baby."

A review of this historic show reveals that, to say the least, the reviewer was less than enthused by what he witnessed. The *L'Eure Eclair* described Jimi as "a singer and guitar player with bushy hair, a bad mixture of James Brown and Chuck Berry, who pulled a wry face on stage during a quarter of an hour and also played the guitar with his teeth."

The fourth and final date of the mini tour took place in front of several thousand fans at the Olympia in Paris. After the Experience set, which consisted of "Killing Floor," "Hey Joe," and "Wild Thing," Chas Chandler and Jimi Hendrix studied Johnny Hallyday's headlining performance, observing how he was able to manipulate the crowd. These show business lessons were not lost on Jimi.

Back in England, the Experience entered the studio for the first time and recorded "Hey Joe" on October 23. The next day Jimi wrote his first song for his new band, "Stone Free." The day after that the Experience made their London debut at the Scotch of St. James. The pace of life surrounding the Experience was clearly picking up momentum. Word was spreading through the closely knit London underground about

Jimi Hendrix, and he claimed a growing number of followers not only among music fans but among other musicians as well.

The Experience recorded "Stone Free" and "Can You See Me" in early November, then traveled to perform a total of six shows in Munich, Germany. Jimi accidentally developed a guitar-smashing routine when he tossed his guitar back onstage after taking a trip into the crowd. The guitar was already cracked, so Jimi finished it off.

"When he picked it up he saw that it had cracked and several of the strings were broken," Chas Chandler later told *New Musical Express*. "He just went barmy and smashed everything in sight. The German audience loved it and we decided to keep it as part of the act when there was good press about or when the occasion demanded it."

Good press was essential to Chandler's campaign to establish The Jimi Hendrix Experience, and on November 25 a press reception and performance were held at London's Bag O'Nails Club. In England, the weekly music papers are highly influential and can easily make or break careers. Chandler's investment paid off with a highly complimentary story and interview that ran in *Record Mirror* under the breathless headline "Mr. Phenomenon!"

On December 13, The Jimi Hendrix Experience broke new ground with their first performance for television on the program

Ready Steady Go! Exposure on shows like this one was crucial to success in England, and Chris Stamp and Kit Lambert had in large part persuaded Chandler and Jeffery to go with them and their Track-Polydor deal based on the guarantee of an appearance on *Ready Steady Go!*

The taped performance of "Hey Joe" aired on December 16—the same day the first record by The Jimi Hendrix Experience was released on Polydor, a single of "Hey Joe" b/w "Stone Free."

As the year came to a close, the Experience continued recording and building a live reputation with shows performed before star-studded audiences made up of people like Jeff Beck, Brian Jones, Paul McCartney, and John Lennon.

By New Year's Eve, the "Hey Joe" single had climbed to number twelve on the R&B charts, and was a solid number thirty-eight on the general charts. And at a party at the home of Noel Redding's mother, Margaret, Jimi received the inspiration for one of his biggest hits.

"It was very cold that night," Margaret Redding recalled. "Jimi asked me if it would be all right to stand next to the fire. That's how he got the idea for the song, 'Fire.'"

The story goes that to get to the fire, Jimi had to get past the Reddings' German shepherd. This is allegedly the source of the line, "Move over, Rover, and let Jimi take over."

The year had been an amazing one. It began with Jimmy Hendrix nearly broke in New York, and ended with Jimi Hendrix standing tall as the toast of the London rock and roll royalty. Even Jimi looked back on the twelve months that had just passed in awe.

"It's all happened thanks to Chas and Mike, really," Jimi said in 1967. "They were the ones who really had the faith that I could make it over here. I was hopeful, but not that confident. I was just playing with my own group in Greenwich Village when Chas saw me. He said it would all happen, just like he said. I still find it difficult to believe it's all happened so fast. I'm working so hard, I guess I don't have time to think about it. Once you make a name for yourself, you are all the more determined to keep it up."

Opposite, bottom: Mitch Mitchell, Noel Redding, and Jimi Hendrix (left to right)—The Jimi Hendrix Experience, pictured at the height of their fame.
Above: In earlier days, Redding and Mitchell sported puffier 'dos that mirrored Jimi's hairstyle.

CHAPTER THREE

MONTEREY AND MONKEE BUSINESS

No matter how well things were going for the Jimi Hendrix Experience as 1967 dawned, there were always going to be people who just didn't get it. And not just parents unable to understand the new rock sounds. When the Experience performed in Sheffield in January 1967, they were billed as "The New Weirdo Trio Jimi Hendrick's Experience." So much for stardom.

But one thing the success of the "Hey Joe" single did accomplish was to spur Polydor into giving Kit Lambert and Chris Stamp the green light to proceed with Track Records. The deal to bring Jimi to Track, with Chas Chandler and Mike Jeffery representing the Experience, was signed on January 11.

Meanwhile the Experience themselves were busy with creative endeavors. Ensconced at the De Lane Lea studio in London, Jimi, Noel, and Mitch were busy laying down tracks that would become hallmarks of rock and roll. The nights were consumed with performances throughout England, with an occasional radio broadcast or interview thrown in for good promotional measure.

Often as not, when Jimi gazed into the crowd from the stage he would see fellow musicians like Jack Bruce and Eric Clapton from Cream or Pete Townshend from The Who staring back in thinly disguised awe. According to Clapton, Bruce was so inspired by what he saw during one Experience show that he went directly home and wrote the main riff to Cream's biggest hit, "Sunshine of Your Love," as a tribute to what he had seen. Ironically, Jimi was unaware of the riff's origins and often performed "Sunshine of Your Love" as a tribute to Cream, one of his very favorite bands.

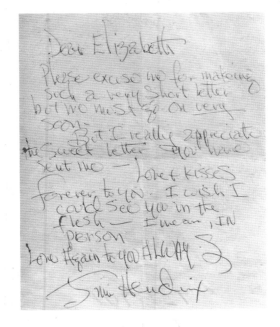

Dear Elizabeth
Please excuse me for making such a very short letter but we must go on very soon... But I really appreciate the sweet letter you have sent me — Love + Kisses forever to you. I wish I could see you in the flesh — I mean, IN person
Love Again to you ALWAYS
Jimi Hendrix

"It's fun to play at little funky clubs, because that's like a work house," Jimi enthused of the packed gigs performed before raving crowds. "It's nice to sweat. I remember we used to play sometimes, even the amplifiers and guitars actually were sweating, everything is sweating. It seemed like the more it got sweaty, the funkier it got and the groovier. Everybody melted together, I guess! And the sound was kicking them all in the chest. I dig that! Water and electricity!"

As much as Jimi enjoyed playing smaller clubs, a look at the horizon showed that those days were coming to an end. With each show it seemed that the audience hysteria was growing. But no matter how great the popularity of The Jimi Hendrix Experience grew to be in England, the real money was waiting to be made across the ocean in America. The task of breaking in a new artist in a country as large as the United States is a daunting one, and both Chas Chandler and Mike Jeffery were well aware of both the difficulty and importance of the job at hand. In January, Jeffery flew to the United States.

Mike Jeffery was something of a mystery man with a reputation for being both shy and brutally tough at the same time. Born in 1933, Jeffery had parlayed a stint in the British armed forces into a

career with the Intelligence Corps. Exactly what he did remained open to conjecture, although stories did circulate that his work involved undercover assignments. Jeffery spoke Russian as well, which added to the cloak-and-dagger aspects of his reputation.

Upon leaving the service, Jeffery went back to school, where he gained experience putting on dances. That led directly to the opening of a group of clubs and an entry into the world of rock management. As manager of The Animals, Jeffery had impressed Chas Chandler with his business intelligence and toughness. Chandler struck up a deal with Jeffery whereby Chandler would get half of the action on the New Animals and another Jeffery property, the Alan Price Set, while Jeffery would get half of the Experience.

Opposite, left: Jimi waits to perform at the Roundhouse on Chalk Farm Road in London on February 22, 1967. Opening for the Experience were The Flies and Sandy & Hilary, acts which have since faded into obscurity. Opposite, right: A letter to a fan offers a peek at Jimi's polite humor. Above, left: Onstage at the Roundhouse, February 22, 1967. Above, right: Experience concerts were frequently opened by Soft Machine; both bands are pictured here in 1967. Jimi later played bass on a solo recording by Soft Machine's Robert Wyatt.

Knowing what they did about Jeffery and his cunning abilities in the field of rock and roll management, it shouldn't have been too surprising to Chas and Jimi that Jeffery returned from his American sojourn with an unprecedented recording contract for Jimi Hendrix. Hendrix was a totally unknown quantity in America, yet Jeffery had landed a $150,000 deal with Warner Brothers that included a most favorable royalty rate and a large advance. Hendrix signed the deal that opened the door to the United States on March 2.

Mike Jeffery wasn't the only rather mysterious character with connections to the British armed forces who traveled in Hendrix's circles. On January 11, Jimi Hendrix met the man who would have a marked impact on Jimi's sound for his entire career.

Roger Mayer was laboring for the Royal Navy Scientific Service when Jimi first met him in 1967. Mayer had a love of the guitar and the mind of an experimenter, which made his association with Hendrix a natural. While Mayer had crafted guitar effects for other musicians, his greatest designs were crafted for Jimi.

One such effect in particular—the Octavia—was given to Jimi on January 27 and became a characteristic tone of the Hendrix sonic palette. An Octavia is capable of creating a second set of notes an

Above, left: Jimi gets down in Paris in 1967. Note that Hendrix would remove the plate that covered the tremolo springs on the back of his Stratocasters so that he could manipulate the springs themselves to create unusual sounds. Above, right: Jimi the celebrity creates a stir among photographers at the London premier of John Lennon's *How I Won the War* in 1967. Opposite: Jimi photographed near his flat at Montagu Square in London in February 1967.

octave apart from those it receives as input, and its remarkable sound helped make Jimi's instrumental voice even more unique.

Interestingly, due to his government work, Mayer could only be credited through pseudonyms. Hendrix often mischievously referred to Mayer as "Roger the Valve." Valve is British terminology for electronic tubes.

"The secret of my sound is largely the electronic genius of our tame boffin Roger the Valve. He has re-wired my guitars in a special way to produce an individual sound and he has made me a fantastic fuzz-tone," Hendrix enthused. "It comes through a whole octave higher so that when playing the high notes it sometimes sounds like a whistle or a flute."

Suddenly Jimi was capable of creating bold, revolutionary sounds when armed with the Mayer effects. Combined with his stunning natural talent, the new technical wizardry gave Jimi the capability to create music unlike any ever heard. The prospect had him excited.

Dear Miss Jennifer
I really appreciate you
taking off time to write
me in this drunk hour
with everything against
us — ENGLE, CAT WALKERS
But we have peace
of mind just as I think
you have. Love always
and forever — Stacy
wait for me —
Jim Hendrix

"There are so many different outlets, you know, we have so many different things. Like 'Hey Joe' is just one little, about one hundredth, you know, of our feelings," Jimi said of the band's first release. "We liked it, that's why we recorded it, you know, but we have so many different other songs that we haven't even... We've just barely begun."

Things continued to progress with the release of the second single by The Jimi Hendrix Experience—and the first on Track

Opposite, top left: The Experience at London's famed Marquee Club in 1967. Opposite, top right: A shot of the Experience at rest, a moment to be savored given their hectic schedule. Opposite, bottom: A letter to a fan, written as Jimi's pen ran out of ink. Above: Another late night in London in 1967.

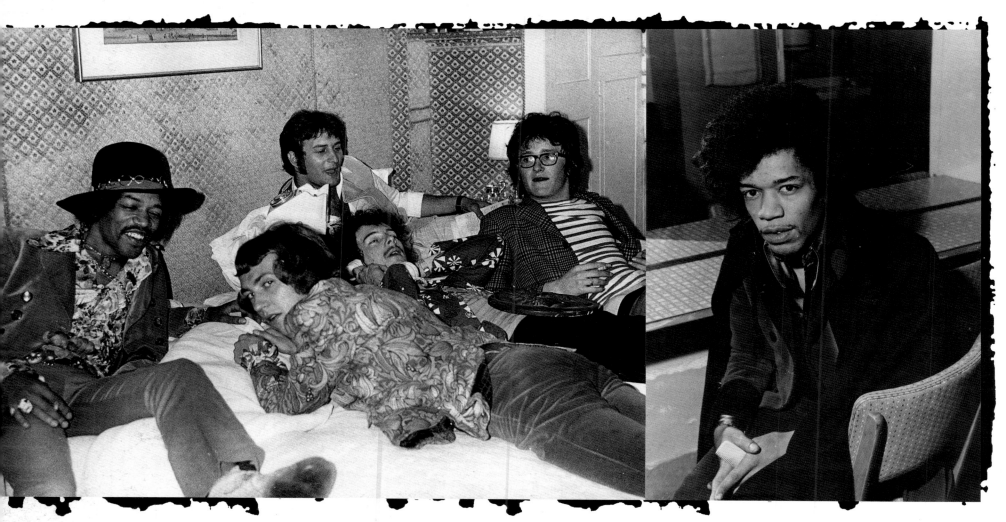

Records—on March 17. "Purple Haze" b/w "51st Anniversary" began a steady climb up the British charts from the moment it was released, eventually peaking at number three.

The month of April was consumed by a full-fledged tour of England in support of the new single. Meanwhile, on May 1, the first Experience single in the United States was released by Warner Brothers. Taking the A-side from the first British single, "Hey Joe," and teaming it with the B-side of the second single, "51st Anniversary," helped reinforce a longstanding and curious tradition of American releases that differ slightly from their British counterparts. But the biggest difference of all was the performance of the American release—it never cracked the Top 40, and it sank into oblivion in the pop charts.

The third Experience single in the United Kingdom—"The Wind Cries Mary" b/w "Highway Chile"—made its appearance on May 5, but the real fireworks began one week later when *Are You Experienced?*, the debut album from The Jimi Hendrix Experience, was released in England.

Are You Experienced? was greeted with rave reviews. In 1967, the significance of a recording artist's work was just beginning to be judged by full-length albums rather than hit singles, and the genius of Jimi Hendrix was best appreciated over lengthier stretches of time. The British music press picked up on that, with the *New Musical Express* raving, "Hendrix is a new dimension in electrical guitar music, launching what amounts to a one-man assault upon the nerve cells."

More important than press approval was the public, which was also sold on the brave new sounds emanating from Jimi's guitar. By mid-June, *Are You Experienced?* was comfortably residing in the number three position. And if it couldn't actually make it to

Above, left: During the Woburn Music Festival, the Experience lounge with friends deejay Emperor Rosko (third from right) and Lord Francis Russell (right), son of the Duke of Bedford, whose presence is indicative of Jimi's magnetism within England's hip society. Above, right: Jimi backstage in 1967.

Are You Experienced?

The term "groundbreaking" is often overused in the music world, but if ever there truly was a groundbreaking album then *Are You Experienced?*, the debut album by The Jimi Hendrix Experience, is it. It stands alongside the greatest recordings of rock and roll, a record with a cataclysmic impact that still echoes through the sounds of today's musicians.

Are You Experienced? not only showed Jimi Hendrix opening a gateway to new possibilities in electric guitar, but it also established the Experience as a new and unexpected force in the rapidly changing rock environment of 1967.

The British version of *Are You Experienced?*, released three months prior to the American equivalent, begins with a song that would become one of Hendrix's signature tunes. Riding in on a billowing wave of feedback, "Foxy Lady" plows straight ahead with a tension-filled, heavy construction. The rhythm and pace of the song are held in check by Mitch Mitchell and Noel Redding, anchoring a track that feels as though it's constantly on the verge of explosion from the first distortion to Jimi's crowning pick slide that finally brings the song to a close.

But that was just the beginning, as *Are You Experienced?* introduced listeners to classic song after classic song. "Fire," "Purple Haze," "Can You See Me," "Manic Depression," "The Wind Cries Mary," and all the other songs associated with the first Jimi Hendrix Experience release covered a remarkable amount of ground, from distortion mania to delicate balladry.

But it's the record's title track that made a lasting statement. "Are You Experienced?" issued the marching orders for the societal upheavals to come. Riding in on Mitch Mitchell's wave of martial beats, the song builds itself with a stately grace. Jimi's weary vocals—surprisingly sober in light of the psychedelic topic—deliver the words in a nearly cautionary tone. The effect is one that is as ominous as it is liberating, as threatening as it is promising.

Are You Experienced? is a landmark recording, the perfect soundtrack to herald the re-invention of rock and roll as an art form.

Above: Hopefully, Jimi's guitar and amplifier were properly grounded. Opposite, left: Jimi chats with Cass Elliott of the Mamas and the Papas. Opposite, right: Hendrix with The Who—Roger Daltrey, Pete Townshend, John Entwhistle, and Keith Moon (left to right)—who shared a bill with the Experience at London's Saville Theatre on January 29, 1967. Months later the Experience and The Who would each perform astonishing sets at the Monterey Pop Festival.

number one, that was okay—the top of the charts was in the grasp of a band that had a bit more experience than the Experience. The Beatles' *Sergeant Pepper* held the top spot.

What wasn't okay was that the Experience hadn't made the slightest of dents in the United States. What was needed was a high-profile platform for the band to make a big splash. In the charmed year of 1967, that's just what The Jimi Hendrix Experience got.

The Monterey Pop Festival was originally planned to be a for-profit festival in California conceived by Alan Pariser and Ben Shapiro. Although they had originated the idea, they were soon shunted to the background when John Phillips of the popular group The Mamas and The Papas and his business manager, Lou Adler, became involved. Adding a high-profile musician board of directors and making the festival a nonprofit affair, Phillips and Adler scheduled the event for June 16 through 18, 1967, at the Monterey County Fairgrounds.

During the planning stages of Monterey, Paul McCartney successfully lobbied festival organizers to book The Jimi Hendrix Experience, a virtually unknown name to American ears.

Before leaving for the United States, the Experience played two last shows at the Saville Theatre. During the song "Are You Experienced?" Jimi smashed one of his Stratocasters, on which he had written a poem that ended:

> True, free expressed music
> My darling guitar
> please rest in peace, Amen

In a small room backstage at Monterey on Sunday, June 17, Janis Joplin, The Rolling Stones' Brian Jones, The Animals' Eric Burdon, and festival coproducer John Phillips looked on as The Who's guitarist, Pete Townshend, and Jimi Hendrix debated the show's running order. The lines were clearly drawn—Townshend did not want to follow Hendrix on stage, and Hendrix did not want to follow Townshend's outfit. Both The Who and The Jimi Hendrix Experience specialized in wild, aggressive performances, and the fact that both bands were to appear as part of the same evening's show guaranteed fireworks.

As Townshend argued, Hendrix stood above him on a chair, effortlessly running through riffs on his Fender Stratocaster. Eventually Phillips was forced to flip a coin to set the running order. Townshend made the right call—The Who would go on first, followed by the Experience. Hendrix stepped down off the chair and, like a

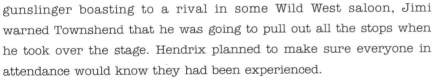

gunslinger boasting to a rival in some Wild West saloon, Jimi warned Townshend that he was going to pull out all the stops when he took over the stage. Hendrix planned to make sure everyone in attendance would know they had been experienced.

Suitably impressed by Jimi's vow, Townshend and The Who took the stage with an explosive set—literally.

The Who had enjoyed little success in America, with the mediocre performance of "Happy Jack" on the pop charts in May 1967 being their best showing. The unsuspecting crowd had little idea that the inconsequential ditty "Happy Jack" was worlds away from the aggression of The Who's live set. They got a rude awakening.

Forty-five minutes after The Who walked on stage, smoke hung over the Monterey festival. Debris was scattered everywhere. Parts of guitars, drums, amplifier cabinets, and microphones littered the once-peaceful stage. The Who had actually blown up before the shocked eyes of tens of thousands of astonished witnesses.

At the end of a high-volume, high-energy set, The Who powered into their furious anthem of alienation and bitterness, "My Generation." At the song's climax, the band switched into auto-destruct mode and Pete Townshend began to violently smash his guitar into the stage floor. Vocalist Roger Daltrey's microphone swung precariously through the air, whistling at a high velocity yet amazingly avoiding contact with any potential victims.

But the real action was about to erupt in the vicinity of the drum kit. Keith Moon, a self-proclaimed loon and one of the greatest drummers in rock's history, was preparing to detonate. According to rock legend, Moon—who had planned on a nice, manageable explosion to drive The Who's set home at the climax of the destruction—had used considerably more explosive material than was necessary to arm himself. When Moon's little explosive device went off, it took Moon's drum kit with it, leaving Moon with a sudden hearing problem and in a decidedly dazed condition.

Opposite: As Jimi's fame grew, photographers seemed to document every waking moment of his day. Above, left and right: The Experience with Jimi at his flat as the threesome continue to push the envelope of fashion.

As the rubble was cleared from the stage, The Jimi Hendrix Experience prepared to make their American debut. In the eyes of American rock fans Hendrix's trio was unknown, since the Experience's debut LP, *Are You Experienced?*, hadn't even been released in the United States yet. Clearly, Jimi's set at Monterey would be crucial to any future plans.

Members of the Hendrix party report that, as he watched The Who's set, Jimi's mood seemed to change from one of nervousness to intensity. What nobody could guess was that Hendrix had decided to deploy some pyrotechnics of his own.

The Rolling Stones' Brian Jones, who had become familiar with Hendrix in England, had the honor of introducing The Jimi Hendrix Experience to America. Polite applause rippled toward the stage and suddenly collided with an immense tidal wave of sound cascading toward the back of the arena.

Silhouetted by dim lights, Hendrix ripped into a brain-rattling rhythm pattern that signalled a revved-up cover of Howlin' Wolf's "Killing Floor." Jimi launched the blues standard into a vastly different orbit, and the stunned audience had no choice but to hang on for dear life.

Above: A star is born in America as The Jimi Hendrix Experience blows minds at the Monterey Pop Festival on June 18, 1967. Opposite: The brilliant Experience performance at Monterey was not an isolated incident, as Redding, Mitchell, and Hendrix left a legacy of legendary concerts in the wake of their travels around the world.

As Mitch Mitchell and Noel Redding fell in on drums and bass, the lights came up to reveal Hendrix in all his peacock glory—tight red pants, a ruffled orange shirt, a rainbow-colored jacket, a bright orange boa wrapped around his upper body, and a headband, all topped off by a black Stratocaster that even this early in the set was doing a superb job of blowing the minds of everyone in attendance. The Jimi Hendrix Experience knew that this was their chance to make an instant name in the United States, and they made the most of the opportunity.

Early in the set Hendrix led the band into Bob Dylan's "Like a Rolling Stone," performing it with an electric intensity that matched the bitterness of Dylan's lyrics. Completely at ease with the Monterey crowd, Hendrix even remarked, "Yes, I know I missed a verse—don't worry!" to one member of the crowd in the midst of the lengthy tune.

By set's end the dumbstruck audience had witnessed a textbook display of every trick Jimi had picked up in his years of working the tough R&B roadhouse circuit. He had played guitar behind his back, behind his head, and with his teeth; done somersaults; run his elbow down the fretboard; and generally performed enough guitar gymnastics to ensure he would not be forgotten in light of The Who or anyone else. But Jimi had one more trick up his Strat.

Vaguely announcing his intention to "sacrifice something I really love," Jimi constructed a cloud of grumbling feedback before leading the band into a chaotic cover of The Troggs' "Wild Thing." Several minutes later Hendrix was hovering

over his hand-painted Fender guitar, a stream of lighter fluid splashing across the instrument's pickups. One quick kiss to the guitar's neck and one match later, rock history was made as one of the most enduring images of American popular culture—right up there with Elvis' sneer—was witnessed live and in person by an audience that had undergone one night of serious sensory overload.

The Jimi Hendrix Experience had more than lived up to their name, and the Monterey Pop Festival had established Jimi as an instant popular culture legend. Jimi came across as charming, powerful, magnetic, funny, and an absolutely amazing guitar player. From a creative standpoint the Experience couldn't have asked for a better performance, and from a business standpoint Chas Chandler and Mike Jeffery couldn't have asked for a better entrance into the U.S. market.

The Experience followed the Monterey show with six nights at the prestigious Fillmore West in San Francisco. Things were going smoothly on the Experience's American visit—until Mike Jeffery phoned Chandler from New York.

Jeffery happily announced that he had signed the Experience to a national tour after cementing a deal with Dick Clark. Chandler asked whom they would be touring with, and the answer could not have come as a greater shock. "The Monkees," Jeffery replied.

The Monkees were the first of the manufactured pop groups, predecessors of acts like Menudo and New Kids on the Block.

Designed around their image more than their music, The Monkees' antics on a weekly television show made them hugely popular with the preteen audience. Unfortunately, the preteen crowd wasn't what Jimi was after.

The tour began on July 8, and for the next several days the Experience took the stage and were greeted by thousands of totally perplexed children. Jimi was upset by both the audience and their reaction to his music, and his playing suffered for it. For every reason, it rapidly became clear that this tour just wasn't going to work out.

Dick Clark had agreed to let the Experience off the tour without litigation if things didn't come together, and the Experience played their last Monkees show on July 16. The Experience's publicist, Michael Goldstein, concocted a purely fictional story that outraged parents and a conservative group, the Daughters of the American Revolution, and that led to Jimi's withdrawal from the tour.

"Firstly, they gave us the 'death' spot on the show, right before The Monkees were due on," Jimi told the *New Musical Express*. "The audience just screamed and yelled for The Monkees. Finally they agreed to let us go on first and things were much better. We got screams and good reactions and some kids even rushed the stage. But we were not getting any billing. All the posters on the show just screamed out MONKEES. Then some parents who brought their young kids complained that our act was vulgar. We decided it was just the wrong audience. I think they're replacing me with Mickey Mouse."

Off the Monkees hook, the Experience recorded in the studio and jammed in Greenwich Village before heading off for dates in Washington, D.C., Michigan, and California. From there, they returned to England and almost immediately began reinforcing their popularity with a string of shows at the end of August.

Are You Experienced? was finally released in the United States on September 1, although the tracks had been shuffled. The songs "Remember," "Can You See Me," and "Red House" were dropped in favor of including the A-sides from the first three British singles. The cover art also differed from the British release.

Meanwhile, the Experience were touring through Sweden before returning home for the by-now obligatory string of television appearances, radio broadcasts, and interviews. The band somehow found time for a quick working trip to France in October despite busily laboring at Olympic studios as they recorded the follow-up to their first album.

Joining Jimi and Chas in the creative recording process was a new partner, engineer Eddie Kramer. A native of South Africa, Kramer would remain a key component of Jimi's studio work for Hendrix's entire career and beyond.

"I vividly remember the day I met Jimi," Kramer told *EQ, The Project Recording & Sound Magazine* in 1992. "It was 1967, and Gerry Stickells, the Experience's road manager, came struggling up the stairs to Olympic Studios with a huge Marshall 4×12 amp on his back. Through a deeply reddened face he bellowed, 'Where do you want me to put this?' I was pretty taken aback, seeing all these large Marshall amps come in.

"Jimi arrived shortly thereafter. He was very quiet and shy. I liked him immediately. And although quiet, he was very demanding. It's not often that you see those characteristics combined, but he knew exactly what he wanted in the studio."

Olympic was a new studio at the time, although the band still only had four tracks to record with. Kramer would typically

Opposite: The Experience onstage at a free concert held at The Panhandle in San Francisco's Golden Gate Park on June 25, 1967. Above: Mitch, Jimi, and Noel (left to right) are all smiles as they map out plans for world domination.

Scenes from sound check at Royal Albert Hall, London, November 14, 1967. Jimi checks out Mitch Mitchell's view from behind the drum kit (above left) then gets down to business dialing in his guitar sound (above right). Note that Hendrix used Sound City amplification to supplement his customary Marshalls at this performance (opposite, top). Playing Royal Albert Hall meant playing at home, as Jimi lived in several London flats over the years. Hendrix began 1967 living at Montagu Square (opposite, bottom).

dedicate two tracks to the drums, one to the bass, and one to the rhythm guitar. Working with Chandler as producer, engineer Kramer would mix those four tracks down to two on another four-track recorder, freeing up two more tracks for lead vocals and guitar. This procedure and the quality results that Kramer achieved are quite amazing, especially in light of the fact that recording on at least sixty-four tracks is now commonplace.

Eddie Kramer and Jimi Hendrix were kindred spirits when it came to experimenting in the studio, and Jimi relied on Eddie to help realize the sounds he heard in his head. The results of their collaboration astonished the music world when the second Experience album, *Axis: Bold As Love,* was released by Track Records in England. When the record hit the stores on December 1, the Experience were in the midst of their second major U.K. tour.

"It's made with stereo in mind and I hope everyone can dig it in stereo because that's what it's all about," Jimi told *Melody Maker* just prior

to the album's release. "The album was made over a period of sixteen days and we all helped in producing it.... We've tried to get most of the freaky tracks right into another dimension so you get that sky effect like they're coming down out of the heavens, you know."

The British rock critics had a difficult time finding enough superlatives to express their feelings about *Axis: Bold As Love.*

The Experience finished the year at the massive "Christmas on Earth" show at the London Olympia on December 22, joining The Who, The Move, Pink Floyd, and others for two sets. The next evening, Jimi dressed as Santa Claus for four hundred children at a charity Christmas party.

New Year's Eve found Jimi at The Speakeasy in London. Never one to turn down an opportunity to jam, Jimi Hendrix rang out an amazingly successful 1967 and welcomed 1968 with a thirty-minute rendition of "Auld Lang Syne."

Above, left: Jimi and Mitch studiously prepare for an American radio interview. While the Experience were hugely popular in England, conquering America required a major campaign throughout 1967 and 1968. Above, right: Hendrix would often deliver his vocals with an intensity that belied his shy nature.

Axis: Bold As Love

The best word to describe the second Jimi Hendrix Experience release, *Axis: Bold As Love,* was found in the center of the record's title: bold.

Coming mere months after *Are You Experienced?*, this second album by Jimi, Noel, and Mitch moved in very advanced directions. So rapid was Jimi's development as a songwriter that songs from the first record seemed almost primitive compared to the wonders of *Axis: Bold As Love.*

Beginning with a bizarre alien interview that leads to "Up from the Skies"—a wah-wah–driven shuffle that examines the state of our planet from an extraterrestrial perspective—*Axis: Bold As Love* suddenly leaps skyward with "Spanish Castle Magic," one of Hendrix's most intense and driving songs. With a ringing piano chord tolling like a bell above the fury of the Experience, "Spanish Castle Magic" showed that the energy that had fueled hits like "Fire" and "Purple Haze" was still in ample supply.

Other songs like "Ain't No Telling," "She's So Fine," "Little Miss Lover," and "You've Got Me Floating" further mined the up-tempo veins of the Experience, while "If Six Was Nine" made a musically slinky but forceful case for independence with its lyric "I'm the one who's got to die when it's time for me to die, so let me live my life the way I want to."

But for all the smoke and fury, it was the three slowest songs on *Axis: Bold As Love* that had the greatest impact. Jimi often spoke of his love of ballads, and he showed that his writing was equal to that of any generation's best with "Little Wing," "Castles Made of Sand," and "Bold As Love."

"Little Wing" has become an oft-covered standard, but no one has come close to approaching the subtle mastery of Jimi's solo opening, followed by the song's all-too-brief tour de force of lyrical, emotional guitar work. In just two minutes and twenty-four seconds, Jimi painted a sonic masterpiece.

The shattered lives and unmet expectations that populate "Castles Made of Sand" were in stark and sobering contrast to much of the lyrical content that appeared on albums of this era, and the words Hendrix wrote for this song stand among his most evocative and image-laden. Each tragic vignette ends with Jimi's lone voice and a guitar expressing waves of sadness, as this song offers up blues interpreted in an entirely new way.

The final song on the album, "Bold As Love," begins with a jolt as Jimi shouts, "Anger!" But the song swiftly settles in on another supple foundation of brilliant rhythm guitar, supporting lyrics that tell tales of colors and emotions—all building to a peak of heartfelt guitar soloing that fades and then reemerges in a cloud of phasing painstakingly crafted by Hendrix, producer Chas Chandler, and engineer Eddie Kramer. It was a breathtaking finish to an entirely satisfying second album.

CHAPTER FOUR

TRAVELING MAN

The aura of success that enveloped The Jimi Hendrix Experience had come at a price. The last half of 1967 was consumed by a dizzying succession of recording sessions, television appearances, interviews, concerts, travel, and mixing sessions, plus all the other demands on time that accompany stardom in rock and roll. In one year the Experience had played more than 250 shows and released two albums.

The year 1968 looked to be no less hectic. After all, the Experience were fully expected to capitalize upon the ground broken by their spectacular Monterey Pop performance. The American market was primed for Jimi Hendrix; all he and the band had to do was deliver as they had in Europe.

All those matters were ones of business and success. But to Jimi, the most important success was evaluated in creative terms. The pressures brought to bear on him were building and may help explain a curious incident that happened on January 4, 1968.

The Experience flew into Gothenburg on January 3 for a string of shows in Sweden to start off the year

Following the Gothenburg show, the band returned to the Hotel Opalen at about two o'clock in the morning. No one has put forth a definitive reason why, but Jimi proceeded to smash up his hotel room quite thoroughly. When the hotel manager let himself into the room with a passkey to investigate the commotion, he found the room filled with debris and Jimi on his bed bleeding from his right hand. Mitch Mitchell was also in the room, and Noel Redding recalls having been forced to sit on Jimi in an effort to calm him down.

Two police officers arrived and tried to arrest Jimi, but he resisted. Reinforcements were called in, and eventually it took several officers to subdue Hendrix. Jimi was taken to the hospital to have his hand treated after its excursion through a plate glass window in the hotel room, and he was then ordered to remain in the

country until his court date on January 16. In best rock and roll manager tradition, Chas Chandler avoided any claims for damages by swiftly paying the hotel for the destruction.

When the Experience's Swedish concerts were finished, the band traveled home on January 9, leaving behind Jimi and Chas. The week of rest, broken only by his required daily check-in at the police station in Gothenburg, could only have helped Jimi after several exhausting months of perpetual activity. On January 16, Hendrix was fined nine thousand Swedish Kronar at his court hearing. Chas and Jimi returned to England the next day.

The day before Jimi was fined, *Axis: Bold As Love* was released in America. This time the track listing mirrored its British predecessor. While everyone was hopeful that *Axis* would

Opposite, left: With bandaged hand, Hendrix walks escorted by the long arm of the law in Gothenburg, Sweden, after laying waste to his hotel room. Opposite, right: Jimi in May 1968 in Zurich, Switzerland. Hendrix's rugged tour schedule included much of the most dreaded aspect of life on the road—sitting around waiting. Above: The toll taken by the two hectic years since his discovery by Chas Chandler can be seen as Jimi prepares to perform on *The Lulu Show* on BBC-TV.

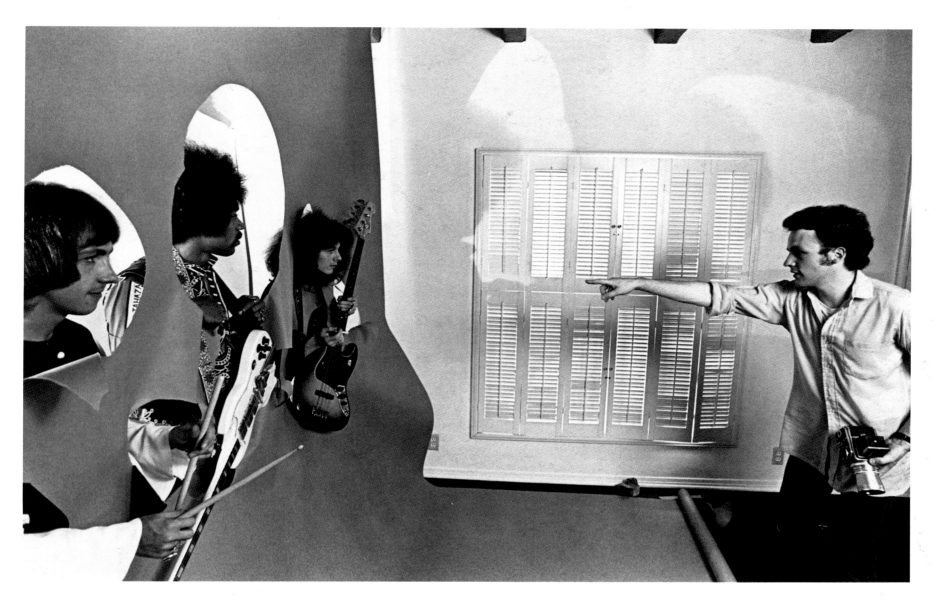

receive the same positive reaction in the United States that it did abroad, of greater concern to the Experience camp was another potential Hendrix release.

Back when Chas Chandler was attempting to buy out all the contracts that Hendrix had signed during his scuffling days, Jimi had failed to mention a three-year exclusive contract signed with Ed Chalpin's PPX record company when Jimi was working with Curtis Knight. On October 15, 1965, Hendrix spent the day in the studio with Knight's band as Chalpin recorded the songs.

In July 1967 word came out that Chalpin was suing Hendrix, Polydor, Track, and Warner Brothers over the contract Hendrix had

signed. Incredibly, after the Experience left the Monkees tour, Jimi had spent two more days in the studio with Chalpin and Knight recording even more material!

Chalpin was legally entitled to release these tracks, and did so beginning with a record titled *Get That Feeling* on Capitol Records. Furthermore, as part of a settlement with Warner Brothers, Chalpin would receive financial interest in the first two Hendrix albums as well as the uncompleted third, and complete rights to the fourth album.

It was a setback, but the main focus in the Hendrix camp was directed at building on the success of the band in America by

The Black Elvis

BY FRANK SIMPSON

NEW YORK, Monday. — The somewhat staid New York Times calls him "a black Elvis." The hippy-oriented Los Angeles Free Press gets a little more ecstatic: "He's an electric religion . . . in a cataclysmic-volcanic-organism finale, we fell back limp in our seats, stunned and numbed."

This, plus sell-out audiences and even a gang of teenage ticket forgers, is the reaction that the Jimi Hendrix Experience gets from its current American tour.

Now, mid tour, Jimi Hendrix has four days off — and needs them. He's relaxing in his hotel room in New York after being thrown out of his first hotel—

means of a lengthy tour. After two warmup shows at the Paris Olympia, the Experience flew directly to New York on January 30.

Publicist Michael Goldstein had arranged a press reception at The Copter Club in New York's Pan Am building, although inclement weather prevented the planned landing of Hendrix and company in a helicopter. Jimi was interviewed by numerous members of the print media and of several radio stations as well.

The stay in New York was brief, as the first date of this important tour was February 1, in San Francisco. The itinerary began with two shows at the Fillmore West, where the Experience played with fellow British bands Soft Machine and John Mayall's Bluesbreakers as well as blues legend Albert King—a man whose playing had influenced Jimi's development.

The next date on the tour was short on travel, as the band simply moved within San Francisco from the Fillmore to three nights at the Winterland Ballroom. The Experience performed two shows each night before heading east to dates in Arizona. After shows in Tempe and Tuscon, it was back to California with performances in Sacramento, Los Angeles, and Santa Barbara. The next stop on the tour: Seattle, Jimi's hometown.

On February 12 the Experience flew from Santa Barbara to Seattle. Waiting at the airport were Jimi's father, Al, who Jimi had not seen in seven years; his brother Leon; Al's new wife, Ayako; and Jimi's stepsister by Ayako, Janie. After a small press reception at Al's home, the family attended the Experience's rather subdued concert at the Center Arena. Jimi then spent the night at his father's house.

The next day, Jimi made an appearance at his old high school, Garfield, where he was supposed to have received a diploma and the keys to the city during a brief ceremony. Unfortunately, it was Lincoln's birthday, and the officials claimed that because of the holiday they were unable to obtain any of the materials to be presented to Jimi.

Opposite: Hendrix delivers another staggering volley of sound, this time in Bakersfield, California, in October 1968. Above, left: Even *The New York Times* was "experienced," christening Jimi "the black Elvis." That news was reported to British fans in this article from *Melody Maker*. Above, right: A Stratocaster's worst nightmare—Jimi in an aggressive mood.

Above: Jimi leans in for a quiet word amid the chaos of life on the road. Opposite, top: The Jimi Hendrix Experience went over big at the Music Hall in Cleveland, Ohio, on March 26, 1968. One member of the audience obviously did not want Jimi to leave. Opposite, bottom: The thought of Hendrix at the wheel always sent a shiver of fear through Jimi's associates. Hendrix was a notoriously bad driver, and the Corvettes that he favored were in as much danger while under his control as Jimi's guitars were.

There was no time to worry about diplomas and keys to the city, as the Experience were off to Colorado, then to Texas. As the tour wound its way back northeast, the band was able to use New York as a base of operations. For Jimi, this meant an opportunity to jam.

While Noel Redding and Mitch Mitchell slipped off to the Bahamas during a brief two-day break from the tour, Jimi remained behind to jam with Eric Clapton. A week later Hendrix jammed with members of The McCoys, joined by a drunken Jim Morrison in a sloppy jam that has become one of the most bootlegged of all Hendrix items. During the tour Hendrix jammed with everyone from the Paul Butterfield Blues Band and The Hollies to Buddy Guy and Roy Buchanan. It was proof that, to Jimi, the guitar was the central component of his professional, recreational, and creative life, and the one thing he never seemed to tire of.

As April gave way to May, the focus turned from road work to studio work. The record companies were already growing anxious for new material—so much so that Track released an album titled *Smash Hits* on April 12. *Smash Hits* was made up mostly of tracks from *Are You Experienced?* joined with the nonalbum singles. The idea was to keep the Hendrix name in the public eye. Warner Brothers would follow suit by releasing an American version of *Smash Hits* just over a year later.

Not that the Experience hadn't been busy recording. During more than a week's worth of sessions at the Record Plant studio in New York, the band labored away at the more complex new material that Jimi was challenging them with. The development of Hendrix's songwriting was maturing at an astounding pace, and the intricate nature of some of the new compositions left some of the early Experience material sounding dated by comparison, mere months after it was recorded. Eddie Kramer had been summoned from England to again work with Hendrix in the realization of his often abstract sonic concepts.

But Jimi was not able to dedicate himself to the studio work entirely, much as he might have liked to. On May 18 and 19 the Experience were booked to perform at the Miami Pop Festival. The first show went well, with Jimi torching another Stratocaster. Torrential rains canceled the second day's show. Instead of heading back into the studio, however, the Experience flew to Milan, Italy, for yet another tour of Europe.

While the Experience were playing in Europe, Mike Jeffery closed a deal to purchase the recently-closed Generation Club on 8th Street in New York. Jeffery and Hendrix initially planned on opening a combination nightclub/recording studio, but saner heads—principally Eddie Kramer—convinced the two men that a studio alone would be the best use of the site.

The fact that Jimi wanted his own studio symbolized the growing changes in his creative process—changes that put a strain on his relationship with Chas Chandler. Where before Jimi had frequently relied on Chas' creative judgement, now Hendrix sought to control his own creative destiny. Jimi began to feel that Chas had an outdated view of the situation.

On the other hand, Chas was bothered by several aspects of the Experience phenomenon that had arisen in the previous year.

Above: Onstage during the Electric Thanksgiving concert at Philharmonic Hall in Lincoln Center, New York City, on November 28, 1968. Opening for Jimi and the Experience were harpsichordist Fernando Valenti and the New York Brass Quintet. Opposite, top: Crowds in the studio were often a hindrance to Jimi when he was trying to fulfill his artistic visions, but this time he put the hangers-on to work at TTG Studios in Los Angeles. Joining Jimi, Noel, and Mitch on October 21, 1968, are several people recruited for crowd noises on "Calling All the Devil's Children," a track that was never officially released. Opposite, bottom: Backstage at the Philharmonic Hall, Jimi was the center of attention in a setting definitely not the norm for rock and roll bands.

Chandler saw the increasing drug use that began to cloak the Hendrix camp as a major problem. This led to additional tension with Mike Jeffery, who seemed to be using drugs to align himself more closely with Jimi. With the ready availability of drugs came a rotating hoard of people just hanging around Jimi, taking up space in the studio and forming a ragtag caravan that followed Hendrix about.

One thing led to another, and during the summer a deal was worked out whereby Chas Chandler's interest in the Experience partnership was bought out by Mike Jeffery. Jeffery would be Jimi's sole manager.

There was also tension forming between Noel and Jimi. With Jimi's burgeoning creativity came a tendency to obsess over every tiny detail of a recording session, leading to marathon mixing sessions trying to resolve imperfections that it seemed only Jimi could hear. Redding had little patience for this nit-picking, and was also disappointed that no interest was being shown in his own material. The fact that Hendrix was interested in using additional musicians on the new material he was crafting just added to Redding's discomfort, as did Noel's growing sense that all was not right in the distribution of profits generated by the Experience.

But the band had no chance to sort any of these growing problems out as they were committed, after another brief European jaunt in July, to yet another American tour in late summer during which they often performed two shows a night. Mike Jeffery's principal interest was in keeping the Experience on the road to generate revenue from the concerts, regardless of Jimi's desire to camp out in the studio.

Given the opportunity, Hendrix could—and probably would—have spent many more hours mixing his next record, but the double album *Electric Ladyland* was finally released in the United States on September 17. The Experience had a brief two-week reprieve from live shows, but the pace picked right back up in early October, most notably with six strong shows over three nights at Winterland in San Francisco.

While once again the new Experience release was welcomed with press raves, Jimi was still dissatisfied with the end result.

"Some of the mix came out kind of muddy, not exactly muddy, but kind of bassey," Hendrix said. "Because we didn't get a chance to do it completely to the end. We mixed it all, you know, and produced it and all this mess, and then when it was time for them to press it, well quite naturally they screwed up because they didn't know what we wanted. There's 3-D sound on there that's been used that you can't appreciate because like they didn't know how to cut it properly. They thought it was out of phase!"

Jimi was also dissatisfied with the British cover of *Electric Ladyland*, which featured twenty-one naked girls. Hendrix claimed that he had never been consulted regarding the British cover of the album. The printing of the cover gave the skin of the young women a rather ghastly greenish hue, making the cover far more of a liability than a selling point. In addition, some stores refused to sell the "pornography."

While concerts like the ones at Winterland were undeniable triumphs, the grind was getting to everyone. Mike Jeffery was counting the money that was flowing in, but nothing was being done about the lifeblood of the Experience that seemed to be leaking out. Rumors began to spread throughout the rock world that the breakup of the Experience was imminent.

The pressure led to incidents like the one on November 30, when Jimi intentionally missed his flight to Detroit for a show at Cobo Arena. Eventually one of Jeffery's key employees, Bob Levine, was able to cajole Hendrix into agreeing to perform. Levine then booked a chartered Lear jet—informing the aviation service that he was calling for Frank Sinatra—which whisked Hendrix to the arena in the nick of time.

Episodes like this one did nothing to soothe the splintering that was going on within the Experience, particularly the strained relationship between Jimi and Noel. But there was hardly time to talk things out or mend fences—the Experience were due in England in early January 1969 for the latest set of European dates.

Above, left and right: Jimi at the Woburn Music Festival in England on July 6, 1968. The Fender Stratocaster Hendrix played that day was built with a rosewood fingerboard, a feature Jimi preferred early in his career.

Electric Ladyland

If *Axis: Bold As Love* was a testament to the burgeoning creativity of Jimi Hendrix, it should have come as no surprise that Jimi's next outlet, *Electric Ladyland,* required the additional room provided by a double album set.

Pages could be devoted to the strengths of *Electric Ladyland,* but several songs in particular must be mentioned when this landmark album is put in perspective.

Enveloping the listener in a smoky, late-night ambiance, the fifteen-minute "Voodoo Chile" finds Jimi relating a story deeply rooted in traditional blues imagery. But Hendrix was known for shattering boundaries, and by the song's end Jimi had used his dark guitar tonality to carve a frightening solo that claimed wholly new territory for the blues.

"1983...(A Merman I Should Turn to Be)" is a fully realized science fiction orchestration. Tapes of Hendrix sketching out the song on acoustic guitar offer proof that Jimi knew exactly what he wanted to do with this track once he got into the studio, and the realization of his plans stands as one of the great achievements of his career. An apocalyptic tale of escape from the surface of a dying planet, the track eerily segues into "Moon, Turn the Tides... Gently, Gently Away" and a lengthy expression of instrumental interpretation before reprising "1983..." in its finale. In 1968 this fifteen-minute-long piece was unprecedented, and today it remains a complex and moving accomplishment.

The songs of Bob Dylan are generally recognized as being difficult to cover due to his distinctive style, but Jimi took Dylan's "All Along the Watchtower" and made it his own. With its unnerving intensity and fiery delivery, Hendrix made this song a milestone of both his career and rock's history. Dylan himself even commented that he liked it better than his original version.

The finale of *Electric Ladyland* was a spiritual cousin of "Voodoo Chile," titled "Voodoo Child (Slight Return)." But on this highly charged electric blues, Hendrix freed his guitar from all constraints, allowing it to roam at will through a shattering deluge of moaning bent notes, tumbling tremolo bar cascades, and runs that burst forth like lightning from clouds of feedback. Above it all, Jimi's voice ominously warned that he had arrived to "stand up next to a mountain, and chop it down with the edge of my hand. I pick up all the pieces and make an island—I might even raise a little sand!" Hearing the astonishing force of this song, it was hard to doubt the validity of Hendrix's boasts.

And having heard the incredible diversity of *Electric Ladyland* as a whole, it was hard to doubt the fact that Jimi Hendrix was now the single most important musician in rock.

STEREO 2612 0 · Polydo · THE JIMI HENDRIX EXPERIENCE ELECTRIC LADYLA

CHAPTER FIVE

CHANGES

The new year was to be one of immense changes for Jimi Hendrix, and appropriately 1969 began with a move as Jimi and Kathy Etchingham set up house in a flat at 23 Brook Street in London. Oddly enough, Kathy and Jimi's home was adjacent to the flat where George Frederic Handel composed "Messiah." (Handel was one of Jimi's favorite classical composers.)

Although together for touring purposes, the supposed breakup of the Experience was now an even hotter topic with the media, particularly with all kinds of rumors shooting through the London music grapevine. The British music papers were involved in a constant game of one-upmanship, and it became quite common to find totally contradictory accounts of the future of the Experience when one newspaper was compared to another.

One thing was certain, and it was a development that added fuel to breakup rumors: Noel Redding had a new band. Including two members of Noel's pre-Experience band The Loving Kind, Fat Mattress was to be a showcase for Noel's material, which had been given little Experience attention. Noel enjoyed playing guitar as a songwriting oulet, and Fat Mattress got him back with six strings rather than four. Mike Jeffery agreed to let Fat Mattress open for the Experience on the forthcoming U.S. tour, meaning Noel would be doing double duty.

"I can't play my guitar any more the way I want to," Hendrix complained early in 1969. "You know, I get very frustrated sometimes on stage when we play. And I think it's because it's only three pieces, you know. I like to work with other things, too, and I'm sure they (Noel and Mitch) would, too, you know. But that doesn't necessarily mean we have to break the group up."

Regardless of the breakup rumors, there was a European tour to be dealt with. January was spent traveling from Sweden to Denmark to Austria to Germany as the Experience logged more road miles. In Dusseldorf, Jimi met a woman who was to play a crucial part in the story of Jimi Hendrix: a young ice skating teacher named Monika Dannemann. Hendrix was fascinated by Dannemann and invited her to several of the shows on the tour.

At the completion of the tour, the Experience geared up for two concerts at the Royal Albert Hall in London on February 18 and 24. Experience shows had been few and far between in England since the big push to conquer the United States began, and these high-profile shows were filmed although never officially released. The performances by the Experience each night were less than spectacular.

The next American tour began on April 11 in Raleigh, North Carolina, before moving on to Philadelphia on April 12. In Philadelphia, rock and roll had found an enemy in Police Commissioner Frank Rizzo, who was determined to keep the hippies in line and regularly raided area rock clubs. The Experience show at the city's largest venue—the newly opened, twenty-thousand-seat Spectrum—became a pep rally of defiance against the oppressive atmosphere.

When the tour hit Memphis, Jimi had a reunion with an old friend, Billy Cox. Confiding that he felt Noel Redding's days with the Experience were numbered, Hendrix gave Cox some money and told him to wait in Nashville for the call to become bandmates once more.

Moving west, the Experience played Los Angeles' Forum. The fact that the band was now playing venues like the Forum and

the Spectrum indicated how successful the Experience were, and they were pulling in tens of thousands of dollars for their sixty-minute sets.

The tour's program was titled *Electric Church: A Visual Experience*. Its title symbolized Jimi's struggle to express the significance of the sounds he heard in his head. Electric Church, Sky Church, Sea Sounds, Valleys of Neptune, South Saturn Delta—all are imagery-laden terms and titles Jimi used to describe different aspects or reflections of his musical personality.

The fact that there was a program for the tour showed the sharp business acumen of Mike Jeffery. Today it's common knowledge that concert merchandising is where bands really make their money, but Jeffery was a pioneer in concert marketing and was one of the first to recognize the importance of such on-site vending.

Above: One of Jimi's few lengthy relationships was with Kathy Etchingham, pictured with Hendrix in their London flat in early 1969. **Opposite:** Jimi began the year 1969 contemplating both the future of the Experience and the new musical directions he was anxious to explore.

But even Mike Jeffery couldn't manage every detail of the tour, and on May 3, disaster struck—Jimi was arrested for drug possession.

When Jimi flew into Toronto early in the morning after his show in Detroit, his flight bag was checked by customs. Inside was found hashish and heroin. Hendrix was charged with possession, taken to police head-quarters, and eventually released on $100,000 bail.

There are various theories as to the origins of the drugs—it was a setup by the police, the small bags of drugs were a forgotten gift from a fan, they were planted in midflight by someone angry at Hendrix—but almost everyone agrees that Jimi was not using heroin. Hendrix remained free pending a trial scheduled for later in the year.

Still, the tour went on. New York, Alabama, North Carolina, West Virginia, Indiana—the Experience crisscrossed the map playing show after show. Jimi managed a few days in the Record Plant studio in New York, jamming with Billy Cox on bass. It was clear to Jimi who would replace Noel

when the time came, but still no announcement was forthcoming. And the tour went on.

Rhode Island, New York City, Baltimore—and then on to the West Coast at the end of May. Despite the exhaustion that must have been setting in and the dread of the potential effects of the drug arrest, the Experience could still deliver the goods when everything was going well. Such was the case with the San Diego show of May 24.

Captured on tape and with the majority of the show released as part of the 1992 live anthology *Stages*, the Experience concert at The Sports Arena not only showed how powerful the band could be but also gave a look at Jimi's personality.

"Hello, how ya doin'?" Jimi asks as he first steps up to the microphone. "Yeah, okay, hold on. Listen, it's going to take us about thirty seconds or forty-five seconds to get ourselves adjusted here and there, little minor things here and there, okay? But before we start we'd like

for you to....Don't concentrate too much on the flashbulbs over there, okay? Let us try to concentrate on a certain thing that we can get across to you and let your money be well spent. (laughs)

"Yeah, okay. Well, like...." As Jimi spots some pushing and shoving with the arena security people: "Hey, leave those people...Hold on, hold on, let's don't get frantic down there — yeah, the cats with the bebop hats, you have to watch out for

them with the flashlights. They're living in the past. (laughs, switches to funny voice) They're living in the past.

"Okay, we'll have to get tuned up and everything. Before we start we'd like for you to for get everything that went on today or last night or things that are supposed to happen tomorrow, because you know we're trying to make our own little world right here. At least give us that. This will be our own electric church, let's say."

A few seconds of unaccompanied guitar, a bit of tuning, and the Experience are now ready to begin for real.

Opposite: Jimi during the preconcert sound check at Royal Albert Hall on February 18, 1969. The London venue hosted two Experience shows that month, both of which were filmed but never officially released. Above, left: Jimi during the second Royal Albert Hall concert on February 24. This was the final European concert by the original lineup of The Jimi Hendrix Experience. Above, right: Mitch Mitchell in the Hit Factory studio in New York in August 1969.

"I'd like to dedicate this song to the girl in the third row with the yellow underwear. Yeah, her," Hendrix jokes, before the band launches into "Fire" with an energy that belies any rumors of impending breakups. Next on the agenda is one of the Experience's oldest songs, but first Jimi must deal with persistent shouted requests for favorite songs.

"Yeah, okay, I'll tell you what, we're going to get into all that," Jimi admonishes. "Don't worry, man, don't worry. You don't have no program, just relax. When I say, 'Toilet paper,' that's when you come rolling out. We'd like to continue on with a thing recorded in 1758 in the Benjamin Franklin Studios, a thing called 'Hey Joe.'"

A slight exaggeration, perhaps, but it must have seemed almost that long ago since the Experience first recorded "Hey Joe" back in October 1966. From there the band goes into "Spanish Castle Magic," complete with a brief foray through Cream's "Sunshine of Your Love" for good measure.

"We call this one the blues," Jimi's next introduction begins, "and we call this one 'Red House.' We're going to do that for a second."

But on this night "Red House" lasts much longer than a second. What follows is a thirteen-and-a-half-minute virtuoso adventure that begins in the blues before traveling to points unknown. The pace is picked up once again by one of Jimi's live favorites, "I Don't Live Today," which climaxes with a guitar freakout and some machine gun–like sounds, which Hendrix files away for future use. "Foxy Lady" comes next, with "Purple Haze," another big hit from *Are You Experienced?*, close behind. But before moving into the song, Hendrix addresses the crowd again.

"Love will not be there in no kind of way unless there's truth and understanding first," Jimi states. "Don't be thrown together by any, 'Come on everybody, let's love together'—that's nothing but a whole lot of hogwash because you have to have truth and understanding in the first place. And this cat, whoever sang this song here, didn't have it in the first place."

Hendrix punctuates his comments by grinding out the repeated two-note intro pattern of "Purple Haze," Noel and Mitch falling in to make the song a lumbering juggernaut of sonic intensity.

Then, it is time to bring the night to a close.

"Thank you and goodnight and peace, peace to you and happiness. Thank you," Jimi says. "And we'd like to say that it was really out of sight to play for ya'll. Here's a song for everybody to grab hold of, not coming from us to you but coming from, you know, just a feeling— self-assurance. A thing called 'Voodoo Child (Slight Return)'—thank you and good night."

So begins the finale, what could be considered Jimi Hendrix's signature song. Rooted in blues, voodoo, and distortion, a feast of bent notes and infinite sustain, "Voodoo Child (Slight Return)" closed many Hendrix sets because there was little else that could follow it.

Despite the strength of shows like the one in San Diego, with the band hurtling along at full flight, the future of the Experience and Jimi's own plans for himself were up in the air.

"We're just getting ourselves together," Hendrix explained. "We're going to play mostly out-side places that hold a lot of people, you know. It'll be like a Sky Church sort of thing. You can get all your answers through music any-way, and the best way is through open air."

Jimi also alluded to using other musicians while giving inter-views during a break in the tour in June, but the band reconvened for a performance at the Newport Pop Festival that was less than stellar. As relaxed as Jimi had been in San Diego, at Newport he was tense and on edge.

"Yeah, we hope we're not playing to a bunch of animals, so please don't act like some," Jimi sniped at one point. "Lay back, okay, because you're really making us uptight, man, you know. It's a bad scene for us to be feeling uptight, try-ing to give you some good feeling and all that sort of crap. I'm just trying to play guitar, thank you."

And then came Denver.

Unlike most festivals, often held far from civilization and with an accompanying lack of amenities, promotor Barry Fey had the logical idea to stage the Denver Pop Festival event at Mile High Stadium, home of professional football's Denver Broncos. With lots of bathrooms and concession stands, theoretically it seemed that little could go wrong.

Opposite: Lost in the studio experience at the Hit Factory in 1969. Above: Due to the popularity of the Experience in the United States, the band played the nation's largest venues on the 1969 tour. Here Jimi mines the ninth fret of his Strat at Madison Square Garden on May 18, 1969.

Unfortunately, everything went wrong. Denver's police force was overrun by thousands of gate-crashers. Members of the Black Panthers and groups made up of ultraradical spin-offs from the just-plain-radical Students for a Democratic Society were determined to establish beachheads at the festival. Fireworks were being set off in the crowd, rocks were being thrown, and fights were everywhere.

Struggling to regain control, the police had regrouped on hills around the stadium. As The Jimi Hendrix Experience played on June 29, the police began launching tear gas into the crowd. Soon the field and the stage were cloaked with the noxious fumes. Through the haze police could be seen in hand-to-hand combat with the audience, and panic swept the crowd.

Hendrix, the band, and the crew fled the stage and jumped into the back of a U-Haul truck, commandeered by Hendrix road manager Eric Barrett, to beat a hasty retreat from the destruction. It turned out that a lot of people thought that was a good idea, and the truck's sides were soon buckled from the weight of concertgoers who had leaped aboard the Hendrix express. Miraculously, the van did not collapse completely, and Hendrix and company were saved from an ignoble fate in the back of a rental truck.

But even more shocking than the armed conflict that gripped Denver Pop was an announcement Jimi had made before complete chaos took over: "This is the last gig we'll ever be playing together." And it was.

"I was planning on leaving Hendrix this year anyway, because I was getting very bored," Noel Redding told *Disc and Music Echo* upon his return to England immediately following the Denver debacle. "And then on our last tour in America, in fact in Denver, we read about Jimi augmenting the band and rumors about me splitting which even I'd never heard about. So I just quit then."

Just two weeks after Denver, Jimi performed on NBC's *Tonight Show* with Mitch Mitchell and Billy Cox. But Jimi still wanted more than the possibilities to be found in a trio. He wanted an expansion of sound, and after moving to a rented house in upstate New York near Shokan, Hendrix set about the task of assembling his collective.

The end result was the short-lived Gypsy Sun and Rainbows band. Jimi was joined by two of his friends from the Nashville days— Billy Cox on bass and Larry Lee on guitar—plus percussionists Jerry Velez and Juma Sultan. Mitch Mitchell was behind the drum kit. The band's first gig? A little gathering known as Woodstock.

While the performance of Jimi Hendrix at Woodstock has become mythical, in reality the Gypsy Sun and Rainbows band was not the most cohesive of units. For much of the set Jimi was forced to cue the band to chord changes or new sections of songs, and Hendrix frequently looked aggravated—which is a shame, because the playing of Jimi himself was masterful. The debut of several new songs was crowned with his now-legendary interpretation of "The Star Spangled Banner" and a brilliant improvisational piece performed solo near the set's end.

Jimi was impressed with the peaceful nature of the Woodstock crowd, but for festivals of the future, Hendrix predicted shows quite similar to the Lollapalooza tours of the 1990s.

Opposite and above: Jimi used stock right-handed Fender Stratocasters to craft his soundscapes, favoring maple fingerboards from 1968 on. Being a left-handed guitarist, he flipped the guitars over and restrung them accordingly. One technical modification performed by Hendrix was to bend the tremolo arms of his guitars to angles he preferred for easier sonic manipulation. The Vox wah-wah pedal was also an essential element of the Hendrix sound.

Above: Early in the morning of August 18, 1969, Jimi Hendrix brought the Woodstock festival to a close. Although Jimi flashed the peace sign from the stage (opposite), he was acutely sensitive to the difficulties faced by the troops in Vietnam. The song "Izabella," performed at Woodstock, was written from the point of view of a soldier far from home fighting "this war for the children and the world and you."

"Woodstock was groovy and all that, but anybody can get a field and put a lot of kids in there and put band after band on," Jimi pointed out. "I don't particularly like the idea of groups after groups. It all starts merging together. They didn't give a damn about the sound equipment, the people way out there that couldn't hear nothing. So when you do festivals, you're either going to have to have more days or offer them things besides music. You know, you should have little booths where they can buy this and that, where the Indians can come and sell their jewelry. A little circus here and there."

Woodstock was one of only three Gypsy Sun and Rainbows performances, with the others taking place at a Harlem benefit and at the Salvation club in Greenwich Village.

Why would a star like Jimi Hendrix play a club in the Village? The story goes that the Salvation club associates, allegedly under Mafia control, "suggested" to Mike Jeffery that Jimi should perform there. Eager to get in the good graces of these associates, Jeffery managed to convince Hendrix to play the gig.

In the weeks between Woodstock and the Salvation club show Hendrix had played in public just once, appearing with Gypsy Sun and Rainbows at a street concert for the United Block Association in Harlem on September 5. Jimi often felt awkward when he was approached by groups like the Black Panthers that wanted him to play up race as an issue, and he did not like the common perception among blacks that he played "white rock for white people." Jimi felt that music was universal and thought the Harlem show would be a good way to spread his music-without-color message. But by the time Hendrix, Mitchell, and company played after midnight, the crowd had dwindled from thousands down to hundreds.

Things didn't go much more smoothly at the Salvation club on September 10. The audience was expecting hits like "Fire" and "Purple Haze" and grew restive with the new, more expansive direction Jimi was taking with the Gypsy Sun and Rainbows band. Overall, the gig was plagued by equipment problems and wound up being a failure, and guitarist Larry Lee soon returned to Tennessee.

The Salvation club also played a part in one of the more bizarre incidents in Jimi's life. Supposedly, Hendrix was kidnapped from the club by lower-level mobsters who wanted to hold him hostage in order to get his contract from Mike Jeffery. Jeffery allegedly used his significant contacts with the Mafia to find out who was responsible for the kidnapping and to secure Jimi's release shortly thereafter. This tale is cloaked in mystery and confusion, with much speculation as to why it occurred or what the details truly were.

Regardless, it added to Jimi's growing paranoia and to his desire to end his relationship with Mike Jeffery. On top of it all, Jimi was at a confusing stage of his career. While he was constantly surrounded by people, very few of them could be trusted as real friends—hence the presence of Billy Cox, an old friend from the prefame days. But Hendrix had a hard time saying no to people, and frequently would let his own needs take second place to those of hangers-on who claimed to be his friends. Studio time was often wasted as recording efforts became unfocused thanks to the gaggle of people who would try to gain access to the studio, much to Eddie Kramer's annoyance.

But Kramer was no longer the sole overseer of Jimi's studio work. Hendrix, through his friend Stella Douglas, had become familiar with her husband, Alan. Alan Douglas had recorded a number of jazz stars like guitar virtuoso John McLaughlin, and those credentials interested Jimi at a time when he was seeking new directions for his music.

Douglas was instantly perceived as a threat by Jeffery, who wanted no outsiders to have the ear of his most prized property.

But soon Douglas began accompanying Hendrix to the studio, alienating Kramer. Eventually, Douglas became what he described as a "consultant" to Jimi regarding business and management issues, naturally adding fuel to Jeffery's anger.

As if there weren't enough upsetting aspects of Jimi's life, his trial on the drug possession charge began in Toronto on December 8. There was no arguing that Jimi had drugs in his bag, but in order for the prosection to gain a conviction they had to prove that Jimi knew the drugs were there. After eight hours of deliberation on December 10, the jury returned a "not guilty" verdict. Jimi described the decision as **"the best Christmas present I could have."**

Despite all these upsetting developments that swirled about Jimi in 1969, he was able to lay down partial or sketch takes of many new songs, and several other new tracks were worked on to near-completion. With Billy Cox on bass, the sound of Hendrix changed significantly. Noel Redding, approaching the bass from the perspective of a guitar player, was much more aggressive and active in his bass lines, particularly in concert. Cox, on the other hand, tended to lay down a much fatter bottom to tracks, with more of an emphasis on smooth funk. It's difficult to say whether one style was better than another—Redding tended to push Hendrix's playing while Cox's bass work intertwined deep within the song rhythms.

At the very end of 1969, however, the Hendrix sound underwent an even more drastic revision. Drummer Buddy Miles was teamed with Billy Cox as Jimi's rhythm section, and the result was an entirely new band: Band of Gypsys.

Opposite, left: Jimi performing with the short-lived Gypsy Sun and Rainbows band in September 1969, following the breakup of the Experience. Opposite, right: Every concert by Hendrix from Woodstock on was supported by the bass work of Billy Cox, one of Jimi's closest friends. Above: One of Jimi's least pleasant appearances—on his way to face narcotic charges in Toronto, Canada, on May 5, 1969. Hendrix's trial, held in December, resulted in a swift "not guilty" verdict.

CHAPTER SIX

THE STORY OF LIFE . . .

"All the hangups of 1969 — kiss my behind."

That was Jimi Hendrix's rather blunt assessment of the year that had just passed, as reported in the New Year's Eve programs distributed at the Fillmore East in New York for the debut of the Band of Gypsys. After the turbulent year that had just ended, it was understandable that Jimi wanted to put it all behind him. Unfortunately, 1970 began to look as though it would be just as chaotic.

But Ed Chalpin was a happy man. He had signed Jimi Hendrix to that exclusive contract when Jimi was playing with Curtis Knight back in 1965, and after suing Jimi's record labels, Chalpin was ready to cash in the settlement he had reached with Warner Brothers. Among other things, the settlement gave him the rights to release the fourth album of new Jimi Hendrix material. After arranging a partnership with Capitol Records, Chalpin sat back and waited to be presented with the lucrative property.

Mike Jeffery looked at the situation as a case of damage control and, since there was no provision forbidding it, decided that the cheapest means of fulfilling the terms of the settlement was for Jimi to turn over a live album of new material. Arrangements were made to record a series of four shows at the Fillmore East.

Although Mitch Mitchell was asked to play with Hendrix at these shows, Mitch had just returned to England after spending almost all of 1969 in the United States. When Mitchell declined the offer, Jimi turned to a good friend, Buddy Miles, to step in. Thus was born the Band of Gypsys: Jimi Hendrix, Billy Cox, and Buddy Miles.

Buddy Miles had drummed with the highly regarded band Electric Flag before forming his own group, the Buddy Miles Express. He and Jimi had become fast friends, with Jimi contributing liner notes to the Express' *Expressway to Your Skull* album and producing several tracks on their *Electric Church* album. Jimi had also jammed with Miles frequently both in private and in public, one time being the two-hour session performed on the second day of the Newport Pop Festival. When Hendrix needed someone to sit in for Mitch Mitchell, Buddy Miles was the logical choice.

For Hendrix, the rehearsals for Band of Gypsys were almost relaxing. In a studio with Cox and Miles, Jimi was among friends, and tapes of the rehearsals reveal that the band was working as they developed new songs but having fun at the same time. At the beginning of the project, Jimi even enthused that Band of Gypsys might be more successful than Gypsy Sun and Rainbows in realizing his vision of a greatly expanded band.

"We would like to plan a tour," Jimi said in late 1969. "We would like to be on the major festivals. We'll play anywhere, where we know it's going to make some kind of penetration or some kind of impact....We're gearing ourselves so we could play anywhere. I might not even be there all the time. Buddy might not even be there all the time, but the core, the whole, the child will be there!"

The Band of Gypsys shows took place on New Year's Eve, 1969, and New Year's Day, 1970, at the Fillmore East in New York. The band performed two shows each night, and theirs was a decidedly different sound than what Hendrix fans had become accustomed to. Whereas Mitchell's drum style when playing with Jimi was very free-form and fluid, Miles tended to lock down the beat and work more with Billy Cox in supporting the song rather than challenging it. This gave Hendrix an extremely solid if predictable foundation from which to launch his playing.

Band of Gypsys was released in April 1970 in the United States and in June in Europe, with all the songs selected from the New Year's Day shows. Ed Chalpin had visions of receiving a studio masterpiece, and was not pleased that he was given a live album, but it met the requirements of his settlement so there was nothing he could do about it—except count the money coming in as the album climbed into the Top Ten. Artistically, Jimi was not especially thrilled with the record, feeling that there had not been enough time to prepare for the shows.

The fifth and final show by the Band of Gypsys was a disaster. Prior to taking the stage at the Winter Festival for Peace at Madison Square Garden on January 28, Jimi was given some bad LSD. Accounts vary regarding who gave it to him or how it was ingested, knowingly or not, but the result was that Jimi was very ill by the time he went on stage at 3 A.M. The band tried to play "Who Knows" from the just-recorded *Band of Gypsys* and a new song Jimi wrote called "Earth Blues." It was no use.

Jimi's playing was beyond control, and before quitting the performance altogether he stepped to the microphone and said, "That's what happens when you're in touch with space. Never forget that." With that, Jimi Hendrix left the stage and Band of Gypsys came to an end.

Later, Jimi commented on what had happened and alluded to the fact that maybe there was more than just bad acid behind what happened.

"It was just something with head changes, going through changes," Hendrix insisted. "It just happened to catch me at that particular time. I

Opposite: Jimi poses for a photograph against a backdrop of advertisements on a London street. Above: Jimi on January 1, 1970, at the Fillmore East in New York. Some of Hendrix's most masterful playing was heard during the four Band of Gypsys shows at the Fillmore, as Jimi felt free to stretch out and concentrate on lengthy musical improvisations.

was very tired. You know, sometimes there's a lot of things that add up in your head about this and that. And they might hit you at a very peculiar time, which happened to be at that peace rally, you know, and here I am fighting the biggest war I ever fought in my life, inside, you know. And like that wasn't the place to do it."

During the Band of Gypsys' brief existence, Mike Jeffery came to the conclusion that he had had enough of Jimi's experiments with his sound. To Jeffery, the bottom line was that things were more easily managed and profitable when he was managing The Jimi Hendrix Experience: Jimi, Noel, and Mitch. With that in mind, he began maneuvers to try to get the threesome back together again.

First Jeffery contacted Noel Redding about returning to the Experience fold. Redding expressed a solid interest. Mitchell had never really strayed far, and was readily available. Besides, Hendrix preferred playing with Mitchell because of Mitch's more adventurous contributions to his material as opposed to Buddy Miles' straight-ahead style.

Jeffery went so far as to arrange an interview with *Rolling Stone* to announce the reformation of the original Experience. Noel then returned to England briefly before the scheduled start of the 1970 American tour. But on March 6, when Noel flew to New York to prepare for the tour, he was greeted with the news that Jimi was now planning to tour with Billy Cox instead.

Cox, Mitchell, and Hendrix passed the time leading up to the tour by recording at the Record Plant. While Ed Chalpin had expected to receive the cream of Jimi's new studio material, in reality Jimi was recording so many new ideas that the vast majority of the tracks he started were not completed. But, contrary to some reports, the time spent in the studio since the release of *Electric Ladyland* was one of intense creativity. Hendrix's ideas encompassed a variety of new directions, and the multitude of studio tapes from this period clearly offer proof of the exciting new directions Jimi's music was taking.

The Cry of Love tour began with a show at the cavernous Los Angeles Forum on April 25, before lumbering onward to Wisconsin, Minnesota, Oklahoma, Texas, and Pennsylvania. But in late May, three dates had to be canceled due to illness. Jimi

Above: Looking down the neck of a Hendrix Stratocaster as Jimi makes the most of some rare quiet time for songwriting. His main concern was writing and recording new material, but manager Mike Jeffery needed to keep Hendrix on the road generating revenue. Jeffery even went so far as to try to arrange a

Band of Gypsys

Ed Chalpin and Capitol Records expected to release Jimi Hendrix's next studio masterpiece, but what they got instead was an album's worth of new material recorded live by Band of Gypsys, the short-lived trio of Hendrix with bassist Billy Cox and drummer Buddy Miles. And while Chalpin and his associates were disappointed with *Band of Gypsys,* in the midst of this uneven recording lies the crowning achievement of Jimi's guitar mastery—and possibly the most brilliant use of the electric guitar ever recorded.

On New Year's Day, 1970, turmoil was the best word to sum up American society. There were riots in the cities, unrest on campuses, and an unpopular war being fought on the other side of the world; the days of peace and love seemed long ago. It was in this atmosphere of anxiety that Jimi Hendrix unleashed his composition "Machine Gun."

For more than twelve minutes, Hendrix used "Machine Gun" to paint an unblinking portrait of the horror of conflict. Using a complex chain of guitar effects—from the Vox wah-wah pedal to the Roger Mayer Axis Fuzz to the Fuzz Face to the UniVibe to the Roger Mayer Octavia—Hendrix became the master of a tone so massive that it remains unequaled today.

The stage was set by Jimi's lyrics of war—"The same way you shoot me down, you'll be going just the same, three times the pain"—before yielding to pure sound as Hendrix began his harrowing journey across a sonic battlefield. Notes cloaked in otherworldly tonal garb arched from Jimi's amplifiers, soaring high and then diving into detonations of grumbling feedback and howling agony. Never does Hendrix's electronic manipulation become mere noise; every disturbing second was a controlled expression that stands as one of the most direct and powerful communications of an artist's deepest visions ever captured in any media.

There is some fine playing by Jimi on the remainder of *Band of Gypsys,* and despite the occasionally overenthusiastic vocals of Buddy Miles, the majority of the album is worth hearing. But even if the rest of the album had consisted of little more than Jimi tuning up, *Band of Gypsys* would climb to the ranks of essential albums because of the presence of "Machine Gun."

had been suffering from swollen glands for some time, and the recurrence of this health problem forced Hendrix to rest.

But when Jimi rebounded from his illness, he did it with a vengeance. Two shows performed on May 30 in the politically charged atmosphere of the Berkeley Community Theater in California stand among the greatest of Jimi's entire career. Both performances were recorded and several songs from the shows have been released, but this evening's concerts are worthy of being made available to the public in their entirety. Film footage of the show, although unfortunately edited, made up the 1971 release *Jimi Plays Berkeley*, which is still available today.

Since the days of the Experience tours, Jimi's sound had undergone further evolution with the utilization of different effects from Roger Mayer and elsewhere. Mayer had further refined his electronics work with fuzz boxes, resulting in the creation of the Axis fuzz. The Octavias Mayer had built, which characterized so many of Jimi's earlier sonic statements, gave way to the UniVibe, a product of UniVox company. After being hot-rodded by Mayer, UniVibes gave Jimi the ability to create "sea sounds." The UniVibe's characteristic ping-ponging signal processing is heard on much of Jimi's work from Woodstock on.

From California it was on to Texas, Oklahoma, Tennessee, Indiana, and Maryland. Then, on June 15, came a moment Jimi had been anxiously awaiting—the opening of his very own recording studio, Electric Lady. Located on 8th Street in New York City's Greenwich Village, Electric Lady had been plagued by cost overruns and construction difficulties—including the unexpected discovery of an underground stream. The project seemed to be a bottomless pit which consumed Experience-generated revenue at an alarming pace.

But at last enough of the work was completed to allow Jimi to actually begin recording in the new studio, which he did on June 15, 16, and 17. But before he could really begin to make himself at home, *The Cry of Love* tour obligations intruded and the band was off to California and Colorado. For the rest of the tour, Jimi would fly back to New York, cram in as much recording as he could, and then jet back out on the road.

On July 4, Jimi played one of the four major festivals at which he would perform in 1970. In front of 500,000 people at the Atlanta Pop Festival, Hendrix performed a set that mixed his earlier hits with newer material like "Message to Love," "Freedom," "Straight Ahead," and "Hey Baby (Land of the New Rising Sun)."

Just two weeks later Hendrix stepped onstage at New York Pop, another three-day festival. Located at Downing Stadium on

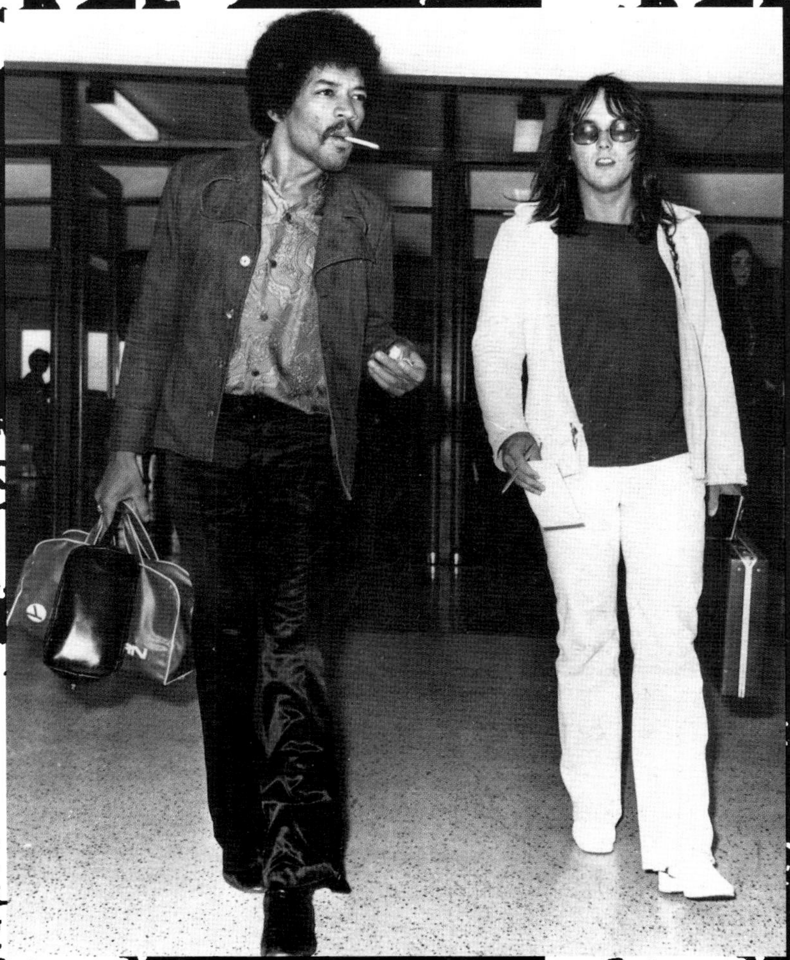

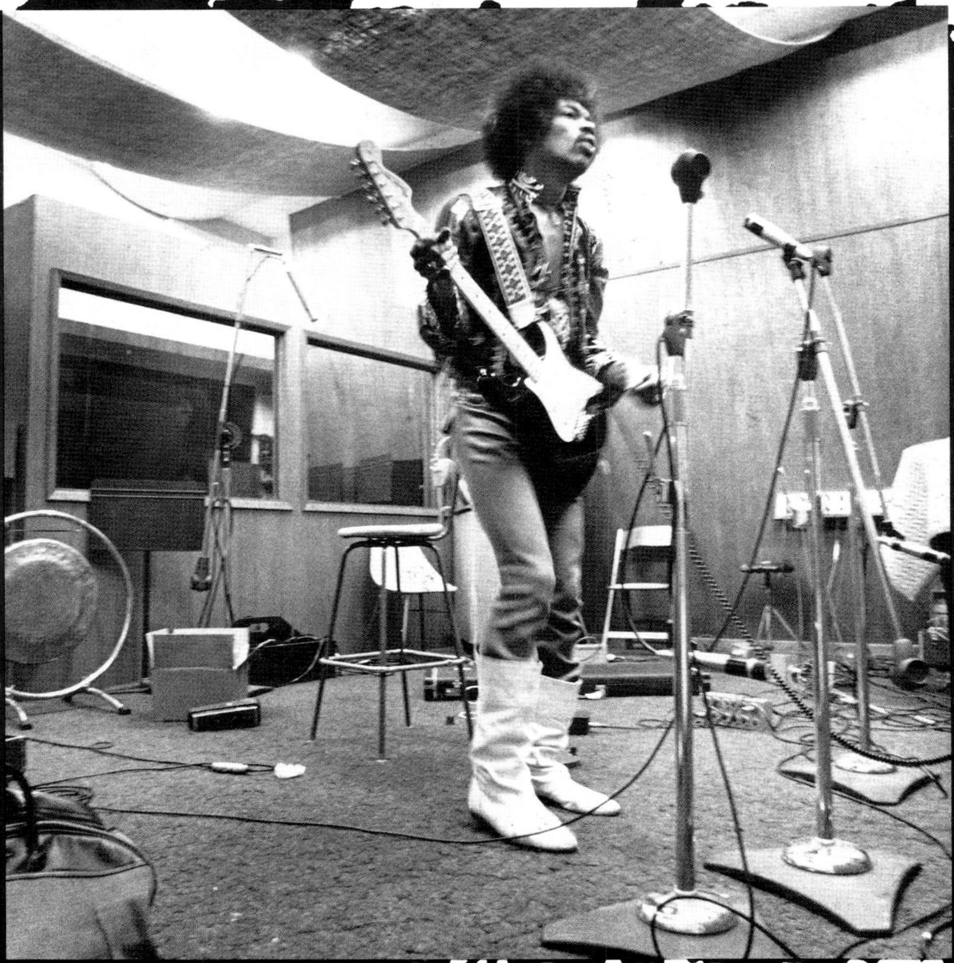

Randall's Island, Jimi performed under chaotic circumstances brought about by the virtual hijacking of festival control by a group of political radicals.

Jimi was able to get in four days of recording from July 20 to 23, and then the tour made its final swing west. After San Diego, Jimi performed again in Seattle. He had a chance to spend some time with his family before pushing onward to the last two dates of the American tour in Hawaii.

Mike Jeffery was fascinated by Hawaii, and in conjunction with director Chuck Wein, he convinced Warner Brothers to put up the money to make a youth-oriented film. Wein, who had been involved in the avant-garde world of Andy Warhol's Factory and insinuated that he was capable of "astral travel," wanted Hendrix in his film and Jeffery delivered. Jimi, Billy, and Mitch performed two sets on July 30 at the Rainbow Bridge Vibratory Color/Sound Experiment, more correctly known as Haleakala Crater on the Island of Maui, in front of a small crowd that numbered in the hundreds, allegedly seated by astrological sign.

When the film was eventually released in 1971 under the title *Rainbow Bridge*, it became clear that the only thing that made any sense in the movie was Jimi's set. The rest of the film was an astonishingly bad, nearly plotless hodgepodge that demonstrated what could go wrong when large corporations, in an attempt to be hip, funded vague and ill-planned ventures.

On August 1 things got back to normal with Hendrix and company performing at the more conventional arena of the Honolulu International Center. This was the last show of the U.S. tour, and was Jimi's last U.S. appearance.

It would have made sense at this point for Jimi to have some time to get together with Eddie Kramer at Electric Lady to begin

Opposite: Jimi Hendrix and Billy Cox recording at the Hit Factory in New York. Above, left: Jimi and road manager Eric Barrett passing through one of the many airports encountered while fulfilling the touring obligations of 1970. Above, right: At TTG Studios in 1968, during the creative peak of the Experience.

Above and opposite, left: Given Jimi's dubious driving skills, the idea of Hendrix at the wheel of a dune buggy may have been more frightening than that of Jimi driving one of his Corvettes. The safest use of this vehicle may have been for gymnastics, a theory Jimi tests during a Hawaiian photo shoot with Ron Rafaelli. Opposite, right: Jimi's last two American concerts took place in Hawaii, the first of which was this one on July 30, 1970, at Haleakala Crater on the Island of Maui.

finishing all the new songs Hendrix had started. Jimi had in mind a two-album set titled *The First Rays of the New Rising Sun.*

But Mike Jeffery was dead-set against a double album. Why use up two albums worth of material in just one release? Besides, he had already committed Jimi and the band to yet another European tour, including a performance at the massive Isle of Wight festival.

Jimi flew to Europe on August 27, the day after a party was held to celebrate the official opening of Electric Lady Studios. Hendrix was reluctant to attend the party in the first place and stayed only briefly. While there, Jimi ran into one of his mates from the Experience, Noel Redding, and told his former bass player that they would get together in London.

In England Jimi did a series of interviews before heading to the Isle of Wight, where another huge crowd of 500,000 had begun gathering on August 26. Playing on the last day of the festival, Hendrix's August 30 performance is generally regarded as falling far short of the standards set by the Berkeley concerts three months earlier. Although buoyed by a passionate "All Along the Watchtower" and a lengthy rendition of "Machine Gun," Hendrix's set was plagued by equipment problems. In particular, the transistors of Jimi's fuzz pedal picked up security walkie-talkie communications and transmitted them down the guitar cable along with the instrument signals. The result was a cacophony of voices continually distracting both Jimi and the crowd.

From Isle of Wight the band traveled directly to Stockholm, Sweden, where they performed on August 31. The next night, after playing a concert in Gothenberg, Billy Cox was given some acid. The result was a tremendous case of paranoia that lasted for days

Above, left and right, and opposite: Jimi Hendrix performing at the Isle of Wight festival on August 30, 1970. At Isle of Wight, accompanied by Billy Cox on bass and Mitch Mitchell on drums, Jimi played both his customary Stratocaster and a Gibson Flying V guitar. Unlike Hendrix's Strats, the Flying V was a left-handed model, and Jimi tended to use this guitar on blues songs like "Red House," as he did on this night.

upon days, with Billy firmly convinced that someone was trying to kill him. The tour was taking a turn for the worse.

By the time the entourage arrived in Denmark on September 2, a cold that Jimi had caught had blossomed into a fever. Three songs into the concert in Arhus, Jimi left the stage, unable to play further.

Still the tour pressed relentlessly onward. Jimi traveled to Copenhagen on September 3 in preparation for that night's show. Mitch's wife had just had a baby, and he flew home for a few hours to visit before returning for the concert at The KB Hallen. Mitchell took Billy Cox with him, as Billy was still too upset from the effects of the acid to be left by himself.

September 4, Berlin: Hendrix played the "Super Concert 70" with other well-known bands including Procol Harum, Ten Years After, and Canned Heat. The next morning Hendrix and company boarded a train and traveled to what would be Jimi's last concert, the Love and Peace Festival at the Isle of Fehmarn on September 6.

Love and peace were in short supply at the festival. Feuding motorcycle gangs waged open warfare against each other as high winds howled and torrential rains pelted the crowd. Jimi's set was delayed a full day by the awful weather. The festival was one of misery, cloaked in a mood as gray and grim as the skies above the festival site. This was what Jimi saw before him as he took the stage for the final time.

Still sick and with a bass player who was convinced they would soon be killed, it's a miracle that Hendrix was able to perform at Isle of Fehmarn. Yet perform he did, winning over the battered crowd before ending the set with a powerful "Voodoo Child (Slight Return)" and its lyric "If I don't see you no more in this world, I'll see you in the next one, and don't be late."

Jimi Hendrix finished the song with one last virtuoso salvo, a hail of unaccompanied notes and a final, spiraling climb upward as he released pressure on his Stratocaster's tremolo bar. "Thank you. Goodnight. Peace," Jimi said, and then he was gone.

Arriving back in England that night, Jimi made arrangements for Billy to stay somewhere until he was well enough to take a flight back to the United States to recover in the care of his parents. The remainder of the European tour dates were canceled due to Billy's condition, although Jimi was far from the picture of health himself.

"I really don't know what kind of band to continue with," Jimi admitted at the time. "I think I'll get another small one together, I guess. It's really hard to decide, you know. I'd like

to have both if I could. Like use one for touring and then sometimes I could do another tour with the big one, you know, whatever. But it all depends, you know. It's really hard to know what people want around here sometimes. All I'm going to do is just go on and do what I feel, but like right now I don't...I can't feel anything right now because like there's a few things that's just happened, you know, and so like, I just have to like, lay back and think about it all."

But Jimi had more than just music to think about. Much to Jimi's dismay, Kathy Etchingham, his longtime occasional girl-friend, had married someone else. And upon the cancellation of the tour, both of the other important women in Hendrix's life were in London while Jimi was grappling with his future plans.

One of the women was Monika Dannemann, the ice skater that had so intrigued Jimi early in 1969. Losing Kathy had an impact on Jimi, and Monika alleged that Jimi made it clear he intended to marry her to give his personal life a needed foundation.

But also vying for Jimi's attention was a very different woman, Devon Wilson. Devon was very streetwise, and had

turned a passion for being friends with famous rock stars into something of a career as a member of the trendy jet set. Leaving behind her roots in Milwaukee, Wisconsin, she was generally regarded as being devious and willing to do anything necessary to get her way. In fact, it was as a direct result of knowing Devon that Jimi had met Stella Douglas and, in turn, Alan Douglas. Jimi cast Devon as the vicious title character in the song "Dolly Dagger," and it was a role that Devon relished.

On September 15, Monika accompanied Jimi to Ronnie Scott's club, where former Animals singer Eric Burdon was playing with his new band, War. Here Monika met face-to-face with Devon, who promptly began trying to provoke Monika. Meanwhile, Jimi had intended to jam with Burdon's band. Stories vary regarding what happened, with some saying Jimi wasn't allowed to play because of the condition he was in and others saying Jimi just didn't feel like waiting around for the group to go onstage. The next night Jimi did jam with Burdon and War, according to Dannemann.

What else was going on during that confused time depends on which of several accounts you choose to believe. While the fact that Jimi spent the day of September 16 with Monika seems fairly agreed upon, the night is another story. Despite Monika's assertion that she and Jimi were at Burdon's show that night, Chas Chandler says that Jimi came to him and asked if they could work together again. Jimi told Chas he needed help and additional perspective with his new studio material. Chandler says Hendrix was with him until early in the morning of September 17.

Chandler's account is backed up by the recollections of Eddie Kramer, who says he got a call at the Electric Lady studio in New York from Hendrix that night. Jimi requested that Kramer bring all of the uncompleted tapes to England, although he did not mention Chandler or their plan to begin work at Olympic Studios. Kramer pointed out to Jimi that they had just finished building Electric Lady and that he thought Jimi should work at the new studio. Kramer remembers Hendrix agreeing and saying that he would return to New York on Monday, September 21.

Chandler recalls that, after talking to Kramer, Jimi told Chas that he was going to go back to New York, get the tapes, and return to London.

One thing that is clear is that Hendrix wanted desperately to distance himself from Mike Jeffery. Chandler recalls Hendrix saying that he would be willing to let Alan Douglas help out with management and other affairs but that under no circumstances

Opposite: Jimi Hendrix and his luggage seek transit on the last tour in 1970. Above: Jimi Hendrix walks to the stage at his final concert on September 6, 1970, at the Love and Peace Festival at the Isle of Fehmarn, Germany.

Above: Jimi Hendrix onstage performing his songs for the last time. As Jimi had done countless times in the four years preceding this show at Isle of Fehmarn, he reaches deeply for a note to take the audience to a new level of experience. Opposite: The master at work—Jimi Hendrix navigating an ocean of sound. Hendrix attained heights of creativity other musicians can only dream of reaching.

should Douglas have anything to do with his music. On the other hand, Douglas claims that Jimi asked him to become his new manager. Furthermore, Douglas has claimed that Mike Jeffery asked him to produce Jimi's new music. And even Ed Chalpin, of the PPX/Curtis Knight contract incident, claims Jimi contacted him for business help, a claim substantiated by Monika Dannemann.

The fog of conflicting claims and stories all leads up to Thursday, September 17. Jimi Hendrix spent the day with Monika, with the most significant event being Jimi's call to his lawyer, Henry Steingarten, with instructions to extricate Hendrix from Jeffery's management.

Early in the evening a chance encounter led to Jimi and Monika attending an impromptu gathering with several of Hendrix's fans, including Philip Harvey, the son of a well-known legislator. Later Jimi and Monika returned to her flat at the Samarkand Hotel, where they dined and drank wine. According to Monika, at around 1:45 A.M. on September 18, Jimi decided to attend a party he had been invited to by Stella Douglas and Devon Wilson. Monika claimed that Jimi was going there to tell Devon to stop harassing her, and that Monika was to drop him off and then pick him up in a half hour. But Eric Burdon's wife, Angie, has stated that Jimi arrived in the middle of the evening and seemed aggravated when Monika kept trying to contact him. According to Burdon, Jimi put off Monika several times before finally leaving the party around 3 A.M.

When Jimi arrived back at Monika's flat, she fixed him a tuna sandwich. Jimi drank more wine. In the back of his mind Hendrix must have been conscious that he had a busy day ahead. Several meetings were planned, and the Chalpin/PPX legal action had moved to England. The first court hearing was scheduled to begin in just hours. After talking with Monika until dawn, Jimi Hendrix turned to barbiturate sleeping pills to help him rest. It was a fatal mistake.

Monika awoke after 10 A.M. and shortly thereafter went out to get cigarettes, after noting that Jimi was sleeping normally. Around 11 A.M., Dannemann returned home and discovered Jimi had been sick but still appeared asleep. She tried to awaken Jimi, but he did not respond. A call for an ambulance was delayed until 11:18 as Monika unsuccessfully tried to find the phone number of Jimi's doctor, and then frantically called friends for advice on what to do. As with most of the incidents leading up to this moment, even Dannemann's phone calls are recalled differently. One person Dannemann reached was Eric Burdon, who she claimed advised her not to call an ambulance. Burdon, however, claimed he told her to call for one immediately.

Regardless, it was too late. Years later, the ambulance men who had arrived at the scene would testify that they knew Jimi was gone almost immediately after arriving at Monika Dannemann's flat at 11:27 A.M. When the ambulance carrying Jimi Hendrix arrived at St. Mary Abbot's Hospital, doctors set to work trying to revive Jimi, but they soon realized it was a hopeless task.

Jimi Hendrix was pronounced dead at the age of twenty-seven on September 18, 1970. On his last afternoon of life, Jimi wrote a poem he called "The Story of Life." It ended:

...the story
of life is quicker
than the wink of an eye
The story of love
is hello and goodbye
until we meet again

CHAPTER SEVEN

LOOSE ENDS

"That's why everybody shouldn't get hung up when it's time for you to die, because all you're doing is just getting rid of that old body, you know," Jimi Hendrix said one year before his death. "The same old body you've been having for about, what is it, about seven years."

The body of Jimi Hendrix was buried on October 1, 1970. In addition to Jimi's family, attending the ceremony at Dunlap Baptist Church in Seattle was a group of Hendrix's associates and admirers including Miles Davis, Buddy Miles, Mitch Mitchell, Noel Redding, Johnny Winter, John Hammond, Jr., Devon Wilson, Alan Douglas, Eric Barrett, and Eddie Kramer. Jimi Hendrix was buried in Greenwood Cemetery, where his mother, Lucille, was buried twelve years earlier.

But the story of Jimi Hendrix does not end with his accidental death. The years since Jimi's death have been filled with accusations, posthumous record releases, and seemingly endless legal conflicts—all parts of the battle for control of the legacy of Jimi Hendrix.

Devon Wilson died in 1971, but she had no direct business interests in Jimi's estate. The same could not be said for Mike Jeffery. At a time when practically every business associate of Jimi Hendrix was involved in some type of litigation against another business associate, Mike Jeffery was killed in a plane crash on March 5, 1973.

Al Hendrix had hired a lawyer named Leo Branton to represent him, but there was a tangled web of offshore financial holdings to be straightened out, a task made all the more difficult by the death of Jeffery. And various lawsuits were either still pending or soon to be filed involving Ed Chalpin, Track Records, Warner Brothers Records, Capitol Records, Noel Redding, women who allegedly had children by Jimi, the company that filmed the 1969 Albert Hall shows, and on and on.

Musically, at least, things progressed in a logical fashion after Jimi's death—at first. Before his own death, Jeffery dispatched Eddie Kramer and Mitch Mitchell to the studio to develop an album from the many tapes at Electric Lady, which Jimi had planned to bring to England for his reunion with Chas Chandler. Unfortunately Jimi's vision of a grand double album was scrapped, and the result of Mitchell's and Kramer's work was *The Cry of Love*, released early in 1971.

The Cry of Love benefited from the fact that there were quite a few songs in a nearly completed state, and this album presented Jimi's fans with studio versions of tracks like "Freedom" and "In from the Storm," songs that Jimi had frequently performed live in 1970. Arguably, the album remained close to Hendrix's vision thanks to the involvement of two men who worked closely with him throughout his career.

But when Jeffery asked Kramer and Mitchell to come up with a soundtrack album for the *Rainbow Bridge* film, released in 1971, they had a problem. The best material at Electric Lady

Opposite, left: A stunned Monika Dannemann is assisted by Eric Barrett just hours after Jimi died in London. Over twenty-five years later, on April 5, 1996, Danneman was found dead in her car, overcome by fumes. Monika's death was treated as a suicide, and came just days after she lost a court case with Kathy Etchingham, who objected to her portrayal as a liar in Danneman's 1995 book about Jimi. Opposite, right: The funeral service for Jimi Hendrix on October 1, 1970. Jimi's casket is carried from Dunlap Baptist Church in Seattle. Above: Al Hendrix waits for family members at his son's burial at Greenwood Cemetery in Renton, southeast of central Seattle.

studio had been used, and they needed access to all the tapes in the possession of Warner Brothers, tapes such as those recorded at studios like TTG and the Record Plant. Eventually, all the Warner Brothers tapes—nearly two hundred—were shipped to Electric Lady. Kramer and Mitchell set about the task of figuring out what was on each reel and the state each song was in.

Several tracks deleted from *The Cry of Love* project were joined by newly unearthed versions of songs like "Earth Blues" and "Look Over Yonder." The album was fleshed out by a live version of "Hear My Train A-Comin'" from the 1970 Berkeley concerts. The truth was that when *Rainbow Bridge—Original*

Motion Picture Soundtrack was released late in 1971, it contained nothing from the Hawaiian concerts it was allegedly the sound-track to. All of the work by Kramer and Mitchell was necessary because the actual concert tapes from the volcano crater show in July 1970 suffered from inferior recording.

At the same time that the *Rainbow Bridge* album made its appearance, Europe was also able to pick up a single record titled *Isle of Wight.* Often labeled one of Hendrix's poorer concert efforts, this album does gather the highlights of the Hendrix set at the massive festival, such as a strong "All Along the Watchtower" and "In from the Storm."

The next Hendrix release to see the light of day was the oddly titled *Hendrix in the West,* a live album that did feature more tracks from Berkeley but also crossed the globe to gather material from Isle of Wight and the London Royal Albert Hall shows of 1969, leaving one asking, "Hendrix in the west of what?" But the true highlight of this album was the stunning "Red House" recorded at the San Diego Sports Arena in May 1969. All in all, *Hendrix in the West* did a good job of capturing some truly special moments from Jimi's live catalog.

So far the output since Jimi's death had been of a fairly high consistency, but things changed with *War Heroes* and *Loose Ends,* released in 1972 and 1974, respectively. Jeffery had run out of finished songs to unleash, so now outtakes and jams began to make an appearance. But at least fans were able to hear Jimi at work, playing with the musicians he chose, despite the uneven quality. However, with the death of Mike Jeffery, all that changed.

Alan Douglas, shunted aside by Jeffery's control in the months immediately after Jimi's death, was approached by Warner Brothers to see if something commercial could be salvaged from the tapes that were still unissued and from other tapes in Douglas' possession. Douglas felt that there was potential—if he wiped off the musicians that Jimi had actually played with and brought in session musicians to jam along with Jimi years after his death.

The ghoulish result was the release in 1975 of both *Crash Landing* and *Midnight Lightning.* These two albums doubtlessly stand as the lowest of the low, shameless exhibitions of what depths people in the recording business will sink to when there is a scent of profit in the air.

Douglas' next decision was to display the side of Jimi that steered toward a musical direction outside the confines of rock and roll. *Nine to the Universe* was, however, mostly a reflection of Jimi's proclivity to spend hour after hour jamming in the studio. While the

tracks on the record contained both Jimi and—in a switch for Douglas—the original musicians who played on the jams, Douglas and his production crew felt the need to heavily edit the material into what they felt was a more palatable form. The result was an awkward compromise—a record that was neither a studio Frankenstein like *Crash Landing* or *Midnight Lightning* nor an accurate "warts and all" portrait of Hendrix in the studio. Released in 1980, *Nine to the Universe* never made it into the Top 100 in the U.S. charts.

Mercifully, for the next decade Alan Douglas refrained from further manipulations of Hendrix studio work. An assortment of studio compilations and live recordings continued to be released, with the highlights being the complete 1967 Monterey Pop performance on *Jimi Plays Monterey,* the *Live At Winterland* and *Radio One* sets, and a satisfying overview of Jimi's live work assembled by Douglas on *The Jimi Hendrix Concerts.* All of those recordings received favorable and enthusiastic reviews, in contrast to the outrage that greeted the butchered studio work.

As the age of the compact disc box set arrived, Jimi was the subject of three substantial collections. *Lifelines* is based on a radio show dedicated to chronicling the history of Hendrix, with three discs containing both hits and some tantalizing sound bites of unreleased material. Particularly exciting, though, was the set's fourth disc, capturing the majority of the 1969 Los Angeles Forum show.

Stages consists of four discs, each one dedicated to a specific concert: 1967 in Stockholm, 1968 in Paris, 1969 in San Diego, and 1970 in Atlanta. Despite the curious facts that the songs on *Stages* changed order from the set lists Jimi actually played and some songs that were played at these concerts were not included on the discs, this collection offers a fine overview of different musical phases of Jimi's career.

The third box set, *The Experience Collection,* is a four-disc set chiefly comprised of the remastered-for-the-digital-age versions of

The Cry of Love & Rainbow Bridge

Both released in 1971, *The Cry of Love* and *Rainbow Bridge* contain many of the songs Jimi Hendrix envisioned including on what he planned to be his next double album. After Jimi's death, Eddie Kramer, assisted by Mitch Mitchell, labored to complete the preparations of the material to offer a final portrait of what Hendrix had accomplished and the new paths he was following.

The Cry of Love gathered the prime cuts that were at Kramer's disposal, and as such it compares favorably with Jimi's best material while revealing some new directions that Jimi was exploring.

Among the highlights are tracks like "Freedom" and "Straight Ahead" which are earthier and funkier than the other songs that rely more on the establishment of solid grooves and the deep bottom laid down by bassist Billy Cox. The restrained and atmospheric "Angel" captured a dream Jimi had of his mother and has become another often-covered song, while "Night Bird Flying" is a densely layered nest of guitar work that touches on a wide range of styles. "Drifting" is the album's most delicate song, gliding through an exquisite haze of backward guitar in one of Hendrix's most dreamlike and moving compositions.

While *Rainbow Bridge* had to be filled out with a masterful live "Hear My Train A-Comin'" due to a shortage of nearly completed studio material, there is no lack of quality in what does appear on the record.

"Earth Blues," "Room Full of Mirrors," and "Look Over Yonder" were culled from earlier Experience and Band of Gypsys studio sessions, as was a heavily overdubbed and orchestrated run through "The Star Spangled Banner." The other three studio tracks are from the summer of 1970, including Jimi's wry paean to Devon Wilson, "Dolly Dagger." Jimi's planned double album was to have been titled *The First Rays of the New Rising Sun,* and "Hey Baby (New Rising Sun)" explores some of the themes Jimi had in mind for this never-completed project. Some of the most pleasing moments on *Rainbow Bridge* come during the lovely instrumental "Pali Gap." Although Mike Jeffery concocted the track's title after Jimi's death to give the song a Hawaiian connection, the easy sincerity of the song's performance more than makes up for it.

Comparing *The Cry of Love* and *Rainbow Bridge* to *Are You Experienced?,* it is amazing how much musical ground Jimi covered in just over three years. It also forces one to ask the saddest of unanswered questions: where else would Jimi Hendrix have taken us had he not died so soon?

Are You Experienced?, *Axis: Bold As Love*, and *Electric Ladyland*, along with the greatest hits compilation *The Ultimate Experience*. While the remastering brought a higher clarity to the material, it brought into focus a common problem with upgrading older material.

Simply put, recordings mixed in Jimi's day were conceived and created to be heard on an analog record player, not a digital compact disc player. It's like looking at artwork digitally scanned onto a laser disc—yes, it's clear, but it's not the way the artist intended it to be viewed. To really appreciate the work of Hendrix, Chas Chandler, and Eddie Kramer, a stylus working its way through vinyl grooves paints the real picture of what these men intended us to hear when they created such influential works of art.

At last, in 1994 Alan Douglas treated Hendrix fans to exciting new, unreleased studio material with *Jimi Hendrix: Blues*. Tracing the deep blues roots of Jimi's music, *Jimi Hendrix: Blues* was a complete success.

Anticipation was high later that same year for the release of *Jimi Hendrix: Woodstock*. Unfortunately, Douglas and company chose to release only parts of the Woodstock performance, changing the running order of what was released and even overdubbing hysterically cheering crowd noises. It's doubtful that the exhausted Woodstock crowd did more than applaud politely when Jimi introduced Gypsy Sun and Rainbows percussionists Juma Sultan and Jerry Velez, but on *Jimi Hendrix: Woodstock* the crowd goes absolutely wild at the mere mention of their names. These recording shortcomings, combined with liner notes that were full of facts but difficult to wade through (a shared trait of latter-day Hendrix releases) made *Jimi Hendrix: Woodstock* a disappointment.

All of which led up to 1995's *Voodoo Soup*. For some time speculation was rampant that Alan Douglas was working to put together an approximation of the double album that Jimi had envisioned just before his death, to be titled *The First Rays of the New Rising Sun*. After all, Hendrix had left behind lists of songs he planned on including on the release, which would certainly provide Alan Douglas with some accurate guidance.

Indeed, Douglas was at work in the studio. Unfortunately, he was back to his old tricks, like replacing Mitch Mitchell's drum parts with new overdubs by Bruce Gary, best known for his work with short-lived pop sensations The Knack. Add in the presence of com-

pletely different mixes and other alterations to the source material, and it's clear that *Voodoo Soup* should justifiably take its place alongside *Crash Landing* and *Midnight Lightning* as Alan Douglas at his worst. As most of the tracks on *Voodoo Soup* had appeared in a substantially less altered form twenty-five years earlier on the now out of print *The Cry of Love* and *Rainbow Bridge* records, this release revealed nothing new and served as less a statement of Jimi's vision than of Douglas'.

Above: Jimi Hendrix as cultural icon. As each year passes, Jimi's memory becomes more and more legendary, his face an instantly recognizable image frequently incorporated into art. This work was created by Ian Wright.

Alan Douglas' arrogance and cavalier attitude toward his position as overseer of Jimi's creative legacy was fully displayed in an interview published in the July 1995 issue of *Guitar World.* In one revealing exchange with interviewer Andy Aledort, Douglas noted that what was important to him in 1995 was to manufacture Hendrix material palatable for "the kids."

"I don't believe these kids give a shit about what was happening 25 years ago," Douglas stated. "They're not interested. There's no nostalgia. There's no retrospective attachment. They're only concerned about what they hear right now. And, fortunately, Jimi created enough material so that you can continue to make records that relate to them now. And it's on the basis of the songs, man. I don't care how good Jimi's playing is: if the song doesn't work for them, they're not interested."

As an example, Douglas pointed to the absence of the *Rainbow Bridge* track "Earth Blues" from *Voodoo Soup*, and how he arrived at the conclusion that "it was too dated."

"But, man, my daughter Kirby doesn't give a shit about any of that," Douglas explained. "She's twenty-two years old. She says, 'What are you playing this for, Daddy? That's not great Jimi Hendrix.' And she knows. She can tell me what songs are great Jimi Hendrix, because she will tell me honestly what she is able to relate to."

Countering Douglas, Aledort pointed out, "Many people feel that Jimi's music should be presented as it was when he died."

"We didn't sell four million records last year because I left it the way it was, okay?" Douglas replied. "I'm not interested in nostalgia. I'm not interested in past attachments. And neither

Opposite: Jimi Hendrix has been awarded many honors in the years since his death, but there is no tribute great enough to reflect his staggering musical impact. Above, left: Al Hendrix at New York's Waldorf Astoria Hotel as his son is inducted into the Rock and Roll Hall of Fame in 1992. Above, right: Jimi's star rises in Hollywood, a sure sign of the attainment of legendary status.

was Jimi—nor would he be if he was here now. And he's not here, man. He's not here, and I got the gig."

In July 1995, Douglas' gig began to look a lot less secure. Two years after suing his lawyer of twenty-three years, Leo Branton, as well as a number of Branton associates (including Alan Douglas), Jimi's father, Al Hendrix, regained control of the Hendrix estate and its assets. Hendrix had sued Branton, claiming that he was conned into signing away control of master tapes, copyrights, and the other properties that make up his son's legacy. As a result of the settlement reached in a Seattle federal court, Hendrix agreed to drop the suit against Branton and pay an amount reported to be between $5 million and $10 million to Branton and others in exchange for regaining rights to the music of Jimi Hendrix, worth an estimated $80 million.

What most Hendrix fans want is to hear the music as Jimi played it, and there is no reason to agree with Alan Douglas' theory that today's younger listeners require Jimi's music to be specially manipulated in order for them to enjoy it.

As for the fact that much of the unreleased material is flawed or not complete to the standards that Jimi would have wanted it to meet, there is some validity in thinking that if he were alive Hendrix would not want such unfinished material released. But sadly, Jimi Hendrix is not here to complete that material, and as has been proven more than once, no one is capable of knowing how Jimi would have finished those tracks.

If the songs that are still unreleased are not fully realized masterpieces, they are at the very least the sonic sketches of a master. Even in their rough state, they are fragments of the genius of rock and roll's most important guitarist and artifacts

that should be shared with and treasured by both the fans of Jimi's era and the younger listeners of today.

Grateful Dead fans mourned the loss of guitarist Jerry Garcia in 1995, yet they were fortunate to have had many years to watch, listen, and enjoy Garcia's continually evolving guitar work. But many of Jimi's fans were born after his death, destined never to have the opportunity to see him walk on stage, plug in, and make a little joke before issuing one of his standard concert advisories: "We want to forget about everything that happened yesterday, last night or this morning. Just forget about everything but what's going on down now. It's up to you and it's up to us, too, so let's get our feelings together." And, of course, they'll never have the chance to watch Jimi Hendrix unleash the astonishing music rooted in another dimension that only Jimi seemed able to summon forth.

There is no doubt that Hendrix's music inhabited realms other musicians can only dream of visiting, but perhaps Jimi himself touched aspects of life that most of us never reach. In 1969, Jimi Hendrix was already looking to the millennium.

"There's other moves I have to make now, a little more towards a spiritual level through music," Jimi said. "Some of the vibrations people claim they are getting now, it is true considering the fact that the Earth is going through a physical change soon. I mean, like since the people are part of Earth, they are going to feel it too. In many ways they are a lot of the reason for causing it...."

Above: Artwork by Henri Martinez incorporating Hendrix's Cherokee ancestry. Jimi is posed as a proud warrior, but one who uses a modern weapon—the electric guitar. Opposite: Al Hendrix in 1995, after control of the estate of Jimi Hendrix was returned to his family following a lengthy court battle. The bass guitar pictured is one of the few personal mementos Al has from his son's career.

"The solar system is going through a change soon and it's going to affect the Earth in about 30 years, you know. And I'm not talking about just this room, I'm talking about the earth itself. This room is just a crumb from the crust of the pie. And like, there's no moving from any one land to another to save yourself in that respect....

"Nothing can explain what I'm going to do later on. I will have to use some sort of brand name. So like, I guess I'll call it the spiritual scene. But it's not a hazy thing out of frustration or bitterness that I'm trying to build up. It's out of what's directing me, what I was here in the first place to do. It does mean I am going to strip myself from my identity because this isn't my only identity....

"I see miracles every day now. I used to be aware of them maybe once or twice a week, but some are so drastic that I couldn't explain them to a person or I'd probably be locked up by this time....I'm not better than you in this sense. It's just that maybe I'm not going to say it until a wider range of people see it. It's a universal thought. It's not a black or white thing, or a green and gold thing.... There are a few chosen people that are here to help get these people out of this certain sleepiness that they are in."

Jimi's friend, Billy Cox, summed up his feelings about Hendrix for *Guitar Player*'s Jas Obrecht.

"You know, there are those who come before the public eye, and they are commercialized into the consciousness of the masses," Cox said. "We are told they are popular, and we echo, 'They are popular.' Then there are a few who are so intuitively tuned into the universe that they are still influential, even though they are beyond sight. This is immortality. Jimi Hendrix is immortal. It is exciting to know the world has yet to truly be exposed to the genius of Jimi. Maybe one day the overshadowing that is used by some to cloud his image will be replaced by the man I knew—a child of the universe, a guitar master, a warm and gentle soul."

bibliography

Aledort, Andy. "Electric Landlord." *Guitar World* (July 1995), pp. 59, 178–183.

Brown, Tony. *Jimi Hendrix: A Visual Documentary.* New York: Omnibus Press, 1992.

———. *Jimi Hendrix: In His Own Words.* New York: Omnibus Press, 1994.

Dannemann, Monika. *The Inner World of Jimi Hendrix.* New York: St. Martin's Press, 1995.

Henderson, David. *Jimi Hendrix: Voodoo Child of the Aquarian Age.* New York: Doubleday, 1978; reprint, *'Scuse Me While I Kiss the Sky: The Life of Jimi Hendrix.* New York: Bantam, 1980.

Kramer, Eddie. "My Hendrix Experience." *EQ, The Project Recording & Sound Magazine* (November 1992).

McDermott, John, with Eddie Kramer. *Hendrix: Setting the Record Straight.* New York: Warner Books, 1992.

Mitchell, Mitch, with John Platt. *Jimi Hendrix: Inside the Experience.* New York: Harmony Books, 1990.

Obrecht, Jas. "Billy Cox: 'Jimi Was a Blues Master.'" *Guitar Player* (September 1995), pp. 79–87.

Robertson, John. *The Complete Guide to the Music of Jimi Hendrix.* New York: Omnibus Press, 1995.

Shapiro, Harry, and Caesar Glebbeek. *Jimi Hendrix: Electric Gypsy.* New York: St. Martin's Press, 1990.

suggested recordings

While the five official recordings released during Jimi Hendrix's lifetime are both essential listening and easily obtained in a variety of formats, the years since Jimi's death have seen the release of numerous recordings and compilations that have gone in and out of print. Some of these recommended recordings are difficult to find, but all are worth hearing. Dates, labels, and formats are shown for each title's original release.

Are You Experienced?
   U.K. LP Track 5/67, U.S. LP Reprise 8/67
Axis: Bold As Love
   U.K. LP Track 12/67, U.S. LP Reprise 1/68
Smash Hits
   U.K. LP Track 4/68, U.S. LP Reprise 7/69
Electric Ladyland
   U.S. LP Reprise 10/68, U.K. LP Track 10/68
Band of Gypsys
   U.S. LP Capitol 4/70, U.K. LP Track 6/70
The Cry of Love
   U.S. LP Reprise 3/71, U.K. LP Track 3/71
Isle of Wight
   U.K. LP Polydor 11/71
Rainbow Bridge—Original Motion Picture Soundtrack
   U.S. LP Reprise 10/71, U.K. LP Reprise 11/71
Hendrix in the West
   U.K. LP Polydor 1/72, U.S. LP Reprise 2/72
War Heroes
   U.K. LP Polydor 10/72, U.S. LP Reprise 12/72
Soundtrack Recordings from the Film Jimi Hendrix
   U.K. LP Reprise 6/73, U.S. LP Reprise 7/73
Loose Ends
   U.K. LP Polydor 2/74
Crash Landing
   U.S. LP Reprise 3/75, U.K. LP Polydor 8/75
Midnight Lightning
   U.S. LP Reprise 11/75, U.K. LP Polydor 11/75

suggested films
available on video
cassette and laser disc

The Essential Jimi Hendrix
U.S. LP Reprise 7/78, U.K. LP Polydor 8/78
The Essential Jimi Hendrix Volume Two
U.S. LP Reprise 7/79, U.K. LP Polydor 1/81
Nine to the Universe
U.S. LP Reprise 3/80, U.K. LP Polydor 6/80
The Jimi Hendrix Concerts
U.S. LP Reprise 8/82, U.K. LP CBS 8/82
Kiss the Sky
U.S. CD Reprise 10/84, U.K. CD Polydor 11/84
Jimi Plays Monterey
U.S. CD Reprise 9/86, U.K. CD Polydor 9/86
Live at Winterland
U.S. CD Rykodisc 5/87, U.K. CD Polydor 1988
Radio One
U.S. CD Rykodisc 11/88, U.K. CD Castle
Communications 2/89
Live and Unreleased
U.K. CD Castle Communications 11/89
Lifelines
U.S. CD Reprise 11/90
Live at Isle of Wight '70
U.K. CD Polydor 6/91
Stages
U.S. CD Reprise 2/92, U.K. CD Polydor 2/92
The Ultimate Experience
U.S. CD MCA 11/92, U.K. CD Polydor 11/92
The Experience Collection
U.S. CD MCA 9/93
Jimi Hendrix: Blues
U.S. CD MCA 4/94, U.K. CD Polydor 4/94
Jimi Hendrix: Woodstock
U.S. CD MCA 7/94, U.K. CD MCA 7/94
Voodoo Soup
U.S. CD MCA 4/95, U.K. CD MCA 4/95

Fortunately, fans are not limited to audio sources to appreciate the genius of Jimi Hendrix.

Jimi Hendrix Experience (1967, 33 minutes) captures the Experience as their ascent to stardom began.

Jimi Plays Berkeley (1971, 55 minutes), although heavily edited, shows footage of two of Jimi's strongest performances in 1970.

Rainbow Bridge (1971, 74 minutes) has a wandering plot full of hippie babble, but the payoff comes with a glimpse of Jimi's set at Haleakala Crater on the island of Maui, Hawaii.

A Film About Jimi Hendrix (1973, 102 minutes) provides the best overview of Jimi's career, gathering clips from many important performances and interviewing Jimi's musical associates and family members.

Jimi Plays Monterey (1987, 50 minutes) presents the splendor of one of Jimi's most important shows, the 1967 Monterey festival performance, in a film that is well made and well recorded.

Jimi Hendrix: Woodstock (1994, 57 minutes) offers nearly an hour of Hendrix's set at the legendary festival, and although Gypsy Sun and Rainbows was not one of Jimi's better bands, Hendrix himself was in fine form.

At the Atlanta Pop Festival and *Isle of Wight* have both been available as imports from Japan. Although neither performance was one of Jimi's best, like all footage of Hendrix concerts, these are worth seeing for the moments of brilliance that shine through.

INDEX

photography credits

© AP/World Wide Photos: 56 left, 85, 87, 99, 106 right, 107, 108, 115

© Chris Bain: 41 both, 53, 69, 75 bottom, 93, 110 both

© CSU Archives/EC: 63 top

© Frank Diggs: 97 right

© Everett Collection: 84, 114

© FPG International: 48

© London Features: 2, 28, 45 both, 90; Govert De Roos: 23 right

© Michael McGettigan: 74

© Michael Ochs Archives, Venice, Cal.: © Joel Axelrad: 75 top left & right, 76 left, 78–79 top, 79 bottom left & bottom right; © Harvey Goodwin: 6 top left & bottom left, 6–7 top right & bottom right, 16 left, 17, 18; © Roz Kelly: 30–31 top, 46, 52 left & right, 54–55, 58 left, 58 right top & bottom; © Michael Montfort: 20–21, 23 left, 24, 26 bottom left, 26–27 top, 27 bottom left, 27 right, 59, 60, 61 left, 63 bottom, 65 top left & right, 66 bottom, 82, 92, 95 right, 96, 101, 102, back jacket

© Photofest: 36 top & bottom left, 56 right, 60–61 inset, 72, 97 left

© Popperfoto/Archive Photos: 8, 31 bottom, 35 right, 38 top left, 44 top left, 100, 103, 106 left

© Ray Avery Archives: 10–11, 104–105

© Retna: © Joel Axelrad: 4–5, 86 right, 88–89, 98 left; © Holland: 16 left, 66 top left; © Geoff Howe: 34 left; © Graham Howe: 35 left; © Michael Putland: 40 left, 68 right; © David Redfern: 40 right, 77 left, 83; © Redferns: 112; © Ray Stevens: 22; © Stevenson: 14

© Rex USA, Ltd.: © Jon Bradley: 111; © David Magnus: 12, 15, 19, 29 both, 32–33, 50 bottom left, 66 top right, 109, front cover; © Barry Peake: 43 right

© Star File Photos: © Jim Cummins: 77 left, 78 bottom, 80, 81, 86 left, 94; © Elliot Landy: 62; © Jeffrey Mayer: 64, 65 bottom left; © Petra Niemeier: 34 right, 36 right, 38 left & right, 39, 42; © Chuck Pullin: 113 left; © B. Wentzel: 1, 13, 30 bottom, 43 left, 44 top right & bottom, 47, 49, 57, 68, 73, 76 right, 98 right; © Vincent Zuffante: 113 right

© UPI/Corbis-Bettmann Archive: 70–71, 91, 95 left

© Val Wilmer: 50 top left, 50–51